A Capital Place
The Story Of
Trenton

A
Capital Place
The Story Of
Trenton

By Mary Alice Quigley & David E. Collier

With Contributions by Ellen and Bert Denker,
Sam Graff, and Sally Lane

"Partners in Progress" by Sally Lane

Produced in Cooperation with the Trenton Historical Society
Windsor Publications, Inc., Woodland Hills, California

Windsor Publications, Inc.
History Books Division
Publisher: John M. Phillips
Production Supervisor: Katherine Cooper
Senior Picture Editor: Teri Davis Greenberg
Senior Corporate History Editor: Karen Story
Marketing Director: Ellen Kettenbeil
Production Manager: James Burke
Design Director: Alexander D'Anca
Art Production Manager: Dee Cooper
Typesetting Manager: E. Beryl Myers
Proofreading Manager: Doris R. Malkin

Windsor Publications' Staff for
A Capital Place: The Story of Trenton
Project Manager: Pamela Taylor
Picture Editor: Kevin Cavanaugh
Corporate History Editor: Phyllis Gray
Sales Representative: Hal Brainerd
Editorial Assistants: Patricia Buzard, Judy Hunter, Patricia Pittman
Compositors: Barbara Neiman, Cynthia Pinter
Proofreaders: Jeff Leckrone, Lynn Johnson
Layout Artist: Ellen Ifrah
Production Artist: Beth Bowman

Library of Congress Cataloging in Publication Data

Quigley, Mary Alice.
    A capital place.

    "Produced in cooperation with the Trenton Historical
Society."
    Bibliography: p. 155
    Includes Index.
    1. Trenton (N.J.)—History.   2. Trenton (N.J.)—
Description.   3. Trenton (N.J.)—Industries.   I. Collier,
David E., 1929-   . II. Denker, Ellen. III. Title.
F144.T757Q53   1984   974.9'66   84-5160
ISBN 0-89781-079-1

Frontispiece: Winkler's Band led the passengers when the first electrified car of the Trenton Passenger Railway Company paused at State and Broad for an inaugural photo on May 22, 1892. Courtesy, Trentoniana Collection, Trenton Free Public Library

Title page: Trenton was still a town of churches, shops, and mills, and the fresh river air was still free of factory smoke when this 19th-century lithograph was made. This view shows Trenton as it appeared from Morrisville across the Delaware. The dome of the state capitol is at the far left. Courtesy, New Jersey Historical Society

CONTENTS

To the memory of seven 20th-century
women we gratefully dedicate this
volume. First, to our mothers who made
loving homes in the city:

Laura Williams Collier   1892-1976
Rose Obert Quigley   1898-1983

To those who shared their knowledge and
love of Trenton with us and made it a
capital place because of their lives and
work:

Rosalie N. Dietz   1902-1978
Martha Wills McKenzie   1938-1982
Mary Jane Messler   1893-1976
Rebecca B. Muehleck   1917-1977
Emma Jane Stockton   1942-1979

ACKNOWLEDGMENTS

Many people and institutions have given us their gracious support in gathering the information and illustrations for this history. The Trenton area is richly endowed with museums, libraries, restored historical and architectural structures and local societies, all of which aid in preserving the region's heritage. The enthusiastic responses which greeted our inquiries were consistent proof of the community spirit and loyalty of Trentonians in recording the past and present achievements of the town.

We are indebted to the staff of the Trenton Free Public Library for making available the extensive Trentoniana Collection. The City Librarian, Harold Thompson, thoughtfully loaned us books to serve as our home reference collection. Nan Wright and Richard Reeves made us aware of the indispensable service that Reference Librarians provide to researchers.

The New Jersey State Library provided professional assistance of the highest caliber. Staff members Rebecca Colesar, Bette Barker, and Joan Dittrich made possible the discovery of illustrations and maps appropriate to our topic. Ellen Denker, Assistant Curator of Cultural History at the New Jersey State Museum, provided us entree to the resources of that excellent institution. At the New Jersey Historical Society, the Curator of the Museum, Alan Frazer, was helpful in locating rare color prints of Trenton scenes that could be copied for inclusion in this book.

The Mayor of the City of Trenton, Arthur Holland, who is deeply committed to improving the present and future of Trenton, gave us more than official support. Extensive, accurate information on city planning activities for the last 40 years was generously loaned to us by Rebecca Mitchell.

At the restored and authentically furnished Trent House, the Curator—Charlotte Gulliver—patiently answered questions and stepped over light cords as rooms were being specially photographed.

Cynthia Koch, the Director of the Old Barracks Museum, also provided research material and permitted new photographs to be made of the interior. Information about the Green House in Ewing Township and the Contemporary Club in Trenton was assembled by Violet Cox, the curator of the Contemporary Victorian Museum. Frances McCarthy was a conscientious researcher on Lawrence Township's historic sites.

The carefully documented articles of Trenton Times staffer, Sally Lane, gave insight to the city's past; sports writer Bus Saidt compiled helpful information about local athletes and teams. Information on the quality of life and on civic activities has been gleaned from fascinating conversations with Rosalie Burrows, Veronica Cary, and Daniel George.

TAWA, the local artist's group, was instrumental in obtaining photographic copies of members' paintings, and in documenting their brief but influential history.

Because of the typing skills of Judith Fullerton, Barbara Kramarz, and Phyllis Angelini, our manuscript efforts were turned into a presentable typescript.

Custom photography to illustrate our narrative meant that early morning and evening hours were spent in the company of the skilled and dedicated photographers, Barry Coleman and Don Reichman, who tried to capture just the right pictures to tell this story. Equally skillful were photographers Ronald Cunningham and Joseph Crilley, who worked with careful consideration of the art objects they captured on film. The copying of oversized atlases and pictures was efficiently, courteously, and thoughtfully accomplished by the staff at Leigh Photo Group and the Keuffel and Esser Reprographics Company. Two individuals volunteered to provide additional research when winter weather hampered travel: Frances Myers and Richard Furman quickly mailed us documentary evidence on 18th-century events.

The two other husband-wife teams who worked on this history—Ellen and Bert Denker and Sally Lane and Sam Graff—have our renewed respect as professionals. As colleagues they were a joy to work with—dedicated researchers, thorough, careful, and prompt authors. Thank you for sharing the labor of this book with us.

Finally, to those businesses and organizations whose support helped insure that Trenton would have an up-to-date history, our grateful appreciation.

Mary Alice Quigley
David E. Collier
Trenton, New Jersey

INTRODUCTION

by Jane Burgio

Secretary of State, State of New Jersey

A Capital Place: The Story of Trenton is, among many other things, a vertical slice of history of the United States. The cabins and the riverside gristmill that became a city move in step with the larger enterprise that became a state, and with the spirit and the land that became a nation. Conceived under European royalty, born into the newness of resourcefulness rewarded, and baptized free through the ritual of war, Trenton, New Jersey, United States of America, in its maturity looks back upon a satisfying history of having missed practically nothing.

Nor have the authors of the book, Mary Alice Quigley and David E. Collier. They mark the passage of the Quaker colonists to a place where the soil was fertile and where hardwood forests and porcelain clays bequeathed industry; where water abounded for drink and labor and boats; and where geology bent the tidal Delaware River and laid a flat and direct pathway between those metropolises to come, New York and Philadelphia.

Trenton ferried the river and fished the river; Trenton stabled the horses and fed the travelers; Trenton made the leather that made the shoes; Trenton made the rails and laid the rails and made the laws that govern New Jersey.

Neither in the history of the nation nor in the history of Trenton did matters remain certain and unchanging and serene. Quigley and Collier identify the transition from agriculture and service to industry, from peace to war and back again, from immigration and growth to population dispersal. They reveal in social and economic terms the results of the changes, and at the same time they demonstrate again and again how Trenton continued to be its own city.

It is state government more than any other body of law and action that orders the day-to-day affairs of Americans. *A Capital Place* tells us that Trenton, nearly the oldest of 50 capital cities, displays its association with state government as a proper and prominent facet of its personality.

Quigley and Collier identify Trenton as a small city. In their hands Trenton becomes a measurable city, a city where people know each other, their common heritage, their streets and their buildings. The Capitol Building—second oldest in the nation—is a case in point: classical in architecture—no sheet glass and aluminum facing here—the Capitol is surrounded by lawns and sidewalks rather than fences and sentry posts, and is accessible at street level to visitors including legions of schoolchildren who daily march by the office of the governor. Trentonians regard the Capitol as theirs.

In the two Battles of Trenton General George Washington changed the course of the Revolutionary War and the lasting pattern of history throughout the world. Quigley and Collier in *A Capital Place: The Story of Trenton* have presented us with a continuing picture of the events and the people and the times, the sum of which is the fascinating history of Trenton, New Jersey.

Chapter One

AT THE FALLS OF THE DELAWARE

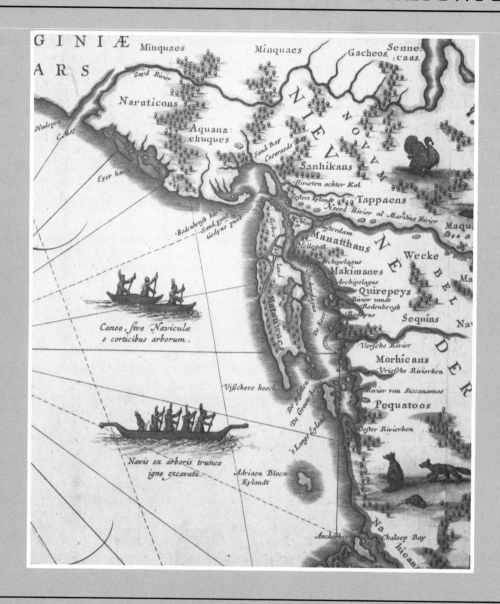

This detail from a 17th-century Dutch
map by Willem Janszoon Blaeu shows
New Jersey lying between the Zuyd
(south) and Noord (north) rivers. The
canoes paddled by Lenni Lenape Indians
are labeled "Navis ex aboris trunco igne
excavata" which means "a boat from a
fire-hollowed tree trunk." Courtesy,
New Jersey State Library (NJSL)

The forces of nature make the falls of the Delaware a logical stopping place for those whose choice of travel is by water. Here the Delaware River runs a shallow course for about two miles. Numerous small islands and obstructing stony outcroppings make navigation hazardous at this point. And the tidal flow ceases at the start of these rocky falls, almost 130 miles from the Atlantic Ocean. This is where the story of Trenton begins: at the falls of the Delaware.

The Europeans, eager to explore the New World, would sail into the broad Delaware Bay between Cape Henlopen and Cape May where they would be enticed inward. At first it was the Swedes and the Dutch, then English adventurers who came to the Delaware River in the 16th and 17th centuries. Although Dutchmen first explored and settled the river banks, their choice of a name, the South River, did not long persist. Neither did their designation for the North River; both, later named after Englishmen, are familiar to us as the Delaware and the Hudson. In 1610, the year after the English Captain Henry Hudson explored the Hudson River Valley in the Dutch ship *Half Moon,* another sea captain, Samuel Argall, sailed from Virginia to check the waterways to the north of that colony. The river which Argall explored was named for Lord De La Warr, the first governor of the Virginia colony. Subsequently, the Indians living along its lower valley were called by Europeans the Delawares, after the river's name.

Although European sailors explored the Delaware's shoreline, the area that was to become New Jersey was sparsely populated for most of the 17th century while it was under Swedish and Dutch rule. Even when the English seized the Netherlands' New World colonies, settlement in the New Jersey area was slow. Conflicting claims that arose out of the uncertainties of English rule were quite complicated. The contradictory claims as to who held the right of government in the region seriously handicapped the ability of the Jersey colonies, East Jersey and West Jersey, to attract settlers.

The British nobleman John, Lord Berkeley, received half of New Jersey as a grant in 1664 from James, the Duke of York (later King James II). Within a few years his grant, western New Jersey, was purchased by a group of middle-class British Quakers. These Quaker proprietors of Berkeley's half of Jersey named the colony West Jersey, and, in 1676, drew up the documents known as the Concessions and Agreements for West Jersey government. The Concessions were circulated at meetings of the Society of Friends in England, Ireland, and Scotland. The framework of government was liberal in nature, with a representative assembly holding the highest power in the colony. Each purchaser of land, and later each inhabitant, had to sign a copy of the Concessions, affirming a willingness to abide by its tenets.

Early in 1677 a group of Quakers was sent to West Jersey to survey the area and locate a settlement site. They established a settlement at Burlington, on the Delaware River, in August 1677. Less than two years later, the first permanent settlement upriver from Burlington would be made at the falls of the Delaware by a small group of settlers led by the Yorkshire Quaker Mahlon Stacy.

With the aid of 20th-century scholarship we can analyze the geography of the area that attracted Mahlon Stacy and his group. Almost in the center of present-day Trenton, near Calhoun Street, the convergence of two physiographic provinces can be found. Here the older rocks of the piedmont foothills disappear below the newer beds of clay, sand, and gravel typical of the inner Atlantic coastal plain. Where these two land forms meet, there is a noticeable change in the river's flow and direction, causing a characteristic waterfall or rapids due to the drop in elevation of the river bed. This pattern is recognizable along the east coast of the United States where it is described simply as the fall line. The Delaware River, flowing approximately 410 miles from its source to the sea, is the most dominant physical feature of the area. The stream flows slowly out of New York State toward Trenton in a southeasterly direction, making an abrupt turn to the southwest after crossing the fall line as it enters the coastal plain. Here the river is affected by the ocean's tide, with the average difference between high and low tide being 4.1 feet at Trenton. The river's mean low-water depth was only five feet until the 20th century when the channel was deepened. With a drainage basin of over 12,000 square miles, the Delaware at Trenton is a good source of power and a constant supply of water, although the early settlers lacked the technology to use it for those purposes, relying instead on individual wells and the river's various creeks.

These creeks were sufficiently substantial bodies of water which were used regularly as municipal boundaries from the earliest English colonization period. The principal creek is the Assunpink, known over the centuries by variations of that name. The Assunpink bisects the

MERCY · JUSTICE

Above: William Penn observed the Lenni Lenape Indians and wrote, "For their persons, they are generally tall, straight, well-built, and of singular proportion; they tread strong and clever, and mostly walk with a lofty chin." The New Jersey Quakers dwelt in peace with the Indians and were concerned with their fair treatment and well-being. Courtesy, Fritz Eichenberg

Facing page top: William Trent bought the 500-acre Stacy plantation of "Ballifield" with 300 adjoining acres in 1714. The confluence of the Delaware River and the Assunpink Creek provided a focus for the beginnings of Trenton.

Oak, maple, and walnut trees mark survey boundaries on this map.

Facing page bottom: As part of the original English settlement at the Falls of the Delaware, Mahlon Stacy built a gristmill on the south bank of Assunpink Creek. The mill was later enlarged by William Trent. This etching, by the noted Trenton artist George A. Bradshaw, was based on a drawing by the historian Lossing, made in 1848 after the mill had been struck by fire and flood. Courtesy, Trentoniana Collection, Trenton Free Public Library (TFPL)

Trenton area as it flows westward to join the Delaware at the falls, and rises 17 miles to the east of the river in Monmouth County. Once again the convergence of the two physiographic regions causes a change in the creek's direction: it actually flows northwest to a point northeast of Trenton where it then bends with the land forms to flow southwest through Trenton.

Two other major creeks, the Shabakunk (in the Ewing Township area) and the Shipetaukin (in the Lawrence Township area), drain into the Assunpink on the northwest. Pond Run and Miry Run unite with the Assunpink on the southeast, before it reaches the city limits. Not apparent to current residents is the rivulet known as Petty's, or Pettit's, Run which has been flumed since the 1890s. It runs from north to south just west of the center of Trenton and, as it approaches the

river, it turns east to join the Assunpink at its mouth. The appellation "Falls of the Delaware" generally applies to the land north, south, and east, extending for several miles around the juncture of the Assunpink Creek to the rocky shallow area of the Delaware River, where the fall line is apparent in a series of rapids, rather than an actual waterfall.

In this century, the Assunpink has a flat and shallow channel; frequently choked by sand, it is prone to flooding and carries muddy water so it is neither a source of water nor a source of power. But its shallowness was an attraction to the early settlers. It could be easily forded and was suitable as a power source for mills, unlike the Delaware River where fluctuations in water level and the height of the banks rendered the simple water wheels of the early settlers inefficient. Those who dared build close to the Delaware were quickly disillusioned by freshets (sudden floods caused by heavy rains or melting snow) such as the ones that occurred in the spring of 1687 and in the winter of 1692 which swept away buildings and cattle as well as European and Indian inhabitants.

Topographically, the Trenton region is a level to slightly undulating plain. Mean sea level is approached at the Delaware's rapids, but the general elevation is between 20 and 60 feet, with an area to the north—the highest elevation—that approaches 100 feet above sea level.

The area's climate was a persuasive factor in European settlement. The long humid summers usually bring about 26 inches of rainfall during the average growing season of 197 days, with the remaining 17 inches occurring throughout the rest of the year. The Yorkshire English, accustomed to a shorter growing season, found the region attractive for the cultivation of grains, vegetables, and fruits. Early farmers were not discouraged by the winter climate, which can be sufficiently severe to freeze creeks and the river; this happens irregularly and then only for a few weeks at a time, usually in January or February.

The land that greeted the Quaker settlers was covered by a broadleaf deciduous forest containing a larger number of species of trees than any other forest area in North America. Primarily of hardwood, the forest made clearing the land for agriculture a problem; however, it did afford a ready supply of wood for home construction and for fuel.

To this attractive new land came first the Yorkshire

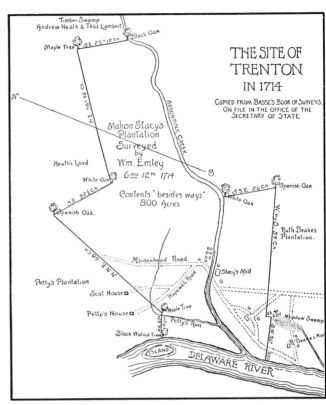

Quakers under the leadership of Mahlon Stacy, George Hutcheson, Thomas Hutchinson, Thomas Pearson, and Joseph Helmsley. This group was assigned 10 shares of West Jersey—one tenth of the total 100 shares. They intended to sell land within their territory to persecuted Quakers in Yorkshire who wished to leave the British Isles yet continue to live in an English country. Hence the Trenton area was referred to, in its early days, as the Yorkshire Tenth, just as other portions of West Jersey were called the Irish Tenth and the London Tenth. The largest group of settlers in the Yorkshire Tenth was from Yorkshire (27). According to a study done by doctoral researcher Stephanie Smith Toothman, another group of 33 came from four adjacent counties in England.

Beginning in 1679, the Yorkshire Quakers opened the West Jersey tract above the Assunpink Creek to permanent European settlers. Mahlon Stacy acquired approximately 3,500 acres of land fronting on the

Delaware and extending eastward inland along the Assunpink Creek to the Shabakunk Creek.

Mahlon Stacy built his house, and a gristmill, near the falls of the Delaware in about 1679. The *Journal of a Voyage 1679-1680* by Jasper Dankers and Peter Sluyter is the first account of the settlement at Trenton by outsiders. Jasper Dankers, a Labadist (Dutch) missionary priest travelling through the area of the falls in the winter of 1679/1680, commented in his journal that Stacy's clapboard house was small, drafty, and so cramped for space that the two visitors could not even find enough room on the floor to sleep and thus were forced to spend the night sitting up. The rude siding let in so much of the November chill that the fire was ineffective. The gristmill, they observed, was made of logs and was not yet completed, and they thought it poorly arranged and likely to fall down if the flow of water was heavy. Despite their negative evaluation, the Labadists noted that the Quakers lived about the new gristmill "in great numbers, and daily increase."

Seven of the men who can be identified from deeds as taking up land near the falls by 1680 arrived together with their families on the ship *Shield* in late 1678. They were, along with Stacy, Peter Fretwell, Robert Murfin, James Pharoe, William Emley, Robert Scholey, and Thomas Revell. Two later land purchasers, Thomas and John Lambert, were also on that ship. This has led at least one Trenton researcher to suggest that these men made plans to establish a settlement even before they arrived in West Jersey. Most of the nine men probably wintered at the already established community at Burlington before moving north to start a settlement at the falls. One, William Emley, wrote from Burlington in 1679:

We are now going to settle a Town at the Falls, at a place reported . . . to be without compare to any other yet known: None equal for pleasant healthful air; Lovely Situation; second to none for Fertility.

There was—and is—considerable truth in his evaluation of the area.

No doubt Mahlon Stacy would have agreed. There was an obvious economic motive in Stacy's letters to England enthusiastically describing the area around the falls. He hoped to entice new settlers and purchasers for some of his vast acreage. Stacy's words painted a picture of a garden spot to welcome the courageous immigrants.

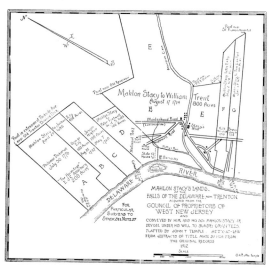

Above: Mahlon Stacy acquired a large tract of land at the Falls of the Delaware from the Quaker Council of Proprietors of West New Jersey. His son sold 800 acres to William Trent in 1714 (marked as "E" on the map). Long strips of land each facing the river were also sold to E. Atterbury, George Ely, Joseph Higbee, Peter Fretwell, William Emley, and Thomas Lambert.

Facing page: Mahlon Stacy and a group of Quakers were the first English settlers at the Falls of the Delaware, and they influenced the initial character of the town. The Friends' Meeting House (seen in this etching by George A. Bradshaw) was built in 1739 and still stands as a place of worship in its original location at the corner of East Hanover and Montgomery streets. George Clymer, a signer of the Declaration of Independence, is buried in the cemetery.

John W. Barber and Henry Howe, in their 1846 *Historical Collections of the State of New Jersey*, quote from Stacy's letter of 1680, which attempts to explain a fruit unknown to the English—peaches:

They are very delicate fruit, and hang almost like our onions that are tied on ropes.

. . . and the good wild fruits:

. . . strawberries, cranberries and hurtleberries, which are like our bilberries in England, but far sweeter: they are very wholesome fruits. The cranberries are much like cherries for color and bigness, which may be kept till fruit come in again; an excellent sauce is made of them for venison, turkeys, and other great fowl; and they are better to make tarts than either gooseberries or cherries.

Stacy continued to praise the goodness to be found at the falls of the Delaware if the settlers were willing to work for it. He wondered at the Yorkshire folk, who would

rather live in servitude to landholding masters, and work hard all year long, year after year, and still be no better off. He wrote that if they would only stir out of their chimney-corners and transport themselves to the Falls, with the same amount of effort they could greatly improve their condition in two or three years.

The newly arrived farmers who examined the soil of Stacy's holdings were pleased that the soil, being generally loamy, could be tilled easily and they could expect a medium to high productivity. The soil averaged three to five feet in depth, and drained well where the lower level was sandy or gravelly. There were patches in lower, flatter areas where there was poor drainage due to the heavy clay subsurface, but generally the virgin soils provided a workable basis for pioneer agriculture. At a later time, this soil would provide a stable foundation upon which to build a city.

Additionally there are various mineral resources close to the surface. Besides the clay, sand, and gravel, there are, for example, pockets of Pleistocene clay (in the Princeton Avenue area) five to six feet in depth which are particularly good for brick and terra cotta production. Along Pond Run are beds of Raritan clay, 10 to 32 feet in depth, under a layer of gravel. About 15 miles to the northwest there is excellent traprock and sandstone suitable for building. These would be significant resources when Trenton later developed into an industrial and governmental center.

But the preeminent factor in the development of the area to the east of the Falls of the Delaware was simply its location. The cities of New York and Philadelphia developed along a geographical line that transects Trenton. There is an easily traversed land connection to New York across the natural lowlands of the inner Atlantic coastal plain, and the area is connected to Philadelphia by river.

By 1700 Philadelphia had emerged as the financial center for the export trade of Pennsylvania and the Delaware Valley—the focus of Quaker energy and capital in America. Philadelphia's rapid growth was based on the Quaker merchants' ability to organize trade networks within the British Empire while remaining largely independent of the London and Glasgow merchants.

The trading activities of West Jersey were quickly overshadowed by those of Philadelphia, and many of West Jersey's most enterprising citizens—men such as Robert Stacy (brother of Mahlon), Samuel Jennings, George Hutcheson, Thomas Hooten, Thomas Budd, Anthony Morris, and Charles Read—moved to Philadelphia. Soon the role of West Jersey was to provide materials such as food or pelts to the Philadelphians, who would then sell them in the city market or ship them abroad. In exchange, Trenton area residents would receive from Philadelphia foreign goods or the products of skilled craftsmen.

While Philadelphia developed as a mercantile center, Mahlon Stacy and his contemporaries preferred to develop a thriving agricultural area. A landing on the Delaware was constructed, probably to handle goods whatever the state of the tides. River and creek transportation was supplemented by paths suitable for a horse or a person on foot. In this way, surplus agricultural products were exchanged for goods, and, just as important, devout Quakers—pioneers in a frontier land—found solace in their attendance at regular meetings.

The members of the Society of Friends were bound together by a system of meetings of varying sizes and purposes, which afforded them flexibility in choosing the location and patterns of their settlements. If members in good standing lived too far from the site of a monthly meeting, they could obtain permission to hold "indulged," or weekly, meetings for worship in their homes.

Permission was granted by the Chesterfield Monthly Meeting in 1685 for the establishment of a weekly meeting near the Falls which met on a rotating basis at the homes of Mahlon Stacy, Thomas Lambert, Samuel Sykes, and William Black. Settling disputes among its members, overseeing the administration of estates, aiding the poor, insuring that marriages were accomplished in an orderly manner, and checking on the morality of its members were other functions of the meeting. The records of the Chesterfield Monthly Meeting present a picture of an essentially stable, almost serene, society in contrast to the confusion and continuous squabbling of the civil government.

Stacy's gristmill at the Falls of the Delaware was the only industry at this site for decades, and, in fact, one of only two gristmills in all of West Jersey. (The other mill, built by Thomas Olive about the same time as Stacy's, was about 20 miles away on the Rancocas Creek.) Farmers for miles around became accustomed to carrying their grain to Stacy's mill. In addition to this rudimentary industry, the germ of a town could also be seen in the type of people attracted to the Yorkshire Tenth. Of middle-class occupations, many had pursued crafts in England. Among the first settlers were two tanners (Robert Stacy and Thomas Lambert), a joiner (John Lambert), and a clothmaker (Robert Scholey.) Mahlon Stacy also ventured into trade as early as 1680. That winter, he, with eight others, bought a two-masted vessel and freighted her for a trip to Barbados, to return to Burlington with salt and Caribbean goods. In writing to England, Stacy boasted that the ship's next freight to the West Indies would be the settlers' own corn. By 1692 the commercial farming economy was sufficiently established to require the West Jersey Assembly to regulate the size of meat barrels and the quality of the contents (the legislative act listed the deleterious effects of bad beef and pork, and short barrels, to the colony's reputation for trade).

By 1702, West Jersey and East Jersey, previously torn by dissension over the right to govern, had been peacefully united as a royal colony. This served to reduce the influence of the Quakers in, for example, the matter of slavery. Queen Anne encouraged the development and growth of slavery. Her orders to the first royal governor of New Jersey directed him to regulate the system of slavery already in existence and to devise a method of increasing the importation of slaves to the colonies. These activities were thought to benefit the Royal African Company of England.

The colonial legislature, in 1713/1714, expressly prohibited slaves, free Negroes, mulattoes, and Indians from owning land anywhere in New Jersey. While slaves were held by some Quakers (usually by the richest third of that group), the Society of Friends was, by the beginning of the 18th century, becoming sensitized to the evils of owning another human being.

The first documented presence of Negro slaves in West Jersey is the 1686 will of Anthony Elton of Burlington who had two slaves together valued at about £40. At least two residents of the Falls area were slave owners: Thomas Smith (died 1702) and Theophilus Phillips (died 1709). Both left instructions in their wills for the freeing of their Negroes, provided that the men serve their widows in good faith for seven years and six

Authentic 18th-century furniture occupies a corner of William Trent's library. A side chair with a cane back stands by the walnut escritoire where a pair of silver spectacles rests on a biography of George Washington and Thomas Jefferson. The Irish bracket clock was made in Dublin by William Marshall in 1740. Courtesy, The Trent House

years respectively. Rebecca Stacy (Mahlon's widow) gave her Negro woman, Jane, her freedom and 20 shillings annually for life. In Nottingham Township, some 16 percent of the area's residents owned slaves during the period 1688-1699. For all of Burlington County (a predominantly Quaker area) it is estimated that 30 percent of its residents owned slaves during the period 1677-1719.

Hunterdon County, formed in 1713, grew faster than any other county in all of New Jersey during the colonial period. It was partitioned twice before the American Revolution into Morris (1738-1739) and Sussex (1753) counties because of the political needs of a burgeoning population. Hunterdon County had itself been formed in 1713 from Burlington County by annexing all the land north of the Assunpink Creek. This included the new townships of Maidenhead (formed in 1696) and Hopewell (1700). Nottingham Township, previously incorporated in 1688, was left in Burlington County. The rivalry between Hopewell and Maidenhead for the county court led to alternating sites, and the issue was finally resolved in 1719 when Trenton Township was formed and designated as the Hunterdon County Seat. It was physically the smallest township in Hunterdon County and it had an illegal southern boundary. Trenton Township was set off by the Hunterdon County Court which scooped up Trent's Bloomsbury, Thomas Lambert's hamlet, and the settlers at Trenton Ferry into the new township—these had all been portions of Burlington County and were not therefore affected by the Hunterdon County partition. They were united for a four-year period (1746-1750) as the Royal Borough of Trenton. The charter was granted by King George II in response to a petition from the Royal Governor, Lewis Morris (a resident of Bloomsbury Court), and a number of other Trentonians. The borough was a political entity that overlapped the functional Trenton area, and, in fact, covered the area described in this history as the "capital place." The royal borough was doomed to failure from the outset because of geographical factors. The roads were too few and in poor condition in an area where the population resided in small clusters; it was simply too large and too unwieldy for efficient borough management. The borough corporation voluntarily surrendered its charter after four years, and the three townships—Maidenhead, Hopewell, and Trenton—reverted to their former status (and former counties).

The year 1719 is significant for it marks the arrival of William Trent, a wealthy Philadelphian, in the affairs of the region around the Falls. Now references begin to appear in official documents to "Trent's Town" and he had a pretty box of a house, built of red brick, constructed on the 300-acre plantation south of the Assunpink Creek, which had been purchased from Mahlon Stacy's heirs. He rebuilt Stacy's frame gristmill in stone. Trent was a prosperous merchant, born in Leith, Scotland in about 1653, who arrived in Pennsylvania in the early 1680s. By 1703 he had become a member of the Governor's Council for Pennsylvania. Trent undertook to develop the town he planned just above the Assunpink Creek at the Falls, but his death in 1724 (at age 71) left it very incomplete. Since he died without a will, his sons Maurice and James tried to fulfill his plans but they both died by 1730, before the elder Trent's estate was settled. Trent's residence, Bloomsbury Court, was sold in 1729 to William Morris, the half-brother of Trent's second wife, who returned to Philadelphia with her minor son. It is worthwhile noting that Trent was an active supporter and member of the Anglican communion, who made his fortune in Philadelphia, the Quaker City, and was influential enough to be elected the Speaker of the Pennsylvania General Assembly in 1718 and 1719.

Trent bought considerable acreage at the Falls, and promoted a town in the small area between the north bank of the Assunpink Creek where the Maidenhead Road crossed the Assunpink (just west of Trent's mills) and the fork created by the convergence of the Maidenhead Road with the Hopewell-Pennington Road—a distance of about half a mile. Three streets form a triangle which is still evident in the city's central core. The base of the triangle is Front Street, which is aligned with the creek: Warren and Broad streets form the sides, all on land set high enough to avoid the river/creek flooding. Trent then sold off small lots of about one-quarter acre each, (principally along Warren Street), and is usually credited with donating the land on which the Hunterdon County Court House was built in 1720. This occurred in only a matter of months after Trenton Township was formed in 1719 (the same year as Trent's arrival) in part to ease the rivalry between Hopewell and Maidenhead townships. The new courthouse was on the east side of Warren Street, located where it would encourage development of the street as a commercial center. The Broad Street area was composed of several small lots with already established businesses such as Hugh Staniland's tavern, which operated prior to 1702. The low-lying land near the river and creek was sold for use as grazing land and orchards, a pattern that was still noticeable 50 years later during the Revolutionary War.

In the triangle of Trent's Town were located the taverns, stores, and churches of the new community. Along the outer fringes were located the major industries: the various mills, the iron and steel works, and the tanning yards. William Yard's tavern, near the intersection of Front and Broad streets, opened prior to 1719 and continued in operation under the management of his son and grandson, with only one brief interruption, until 1775. On the southeast corner of Warren and State streets was the store first kept by Moore Furman, which became known as Furman and Hunt in 1762. This firm carried on an extensive freighting business, via two packet boats manned by Trentonians which ran between Philadelphia and Trenton. Researcher Stephanie Smith Toothman's analysis of the 1773 Tax Rateables for Hunterdon County shows that Trenton Township had the largest number of merchants (12) in the smallest area compared to no merchants for adjoining Maidenhead Township. Also concentrated in the town core were

Above and facing page: Original Delft tiles portraying children's games (shown in detail on facing page) decorate the wide, panelled fireplace of Madam Trent's sitting room. Between the andirons sits a copper bed warmer. A rare Queen Anne overmantle looking glass with two sconces highlights the room's elegance. Courtesy, The Trent House

three buildings erected for religious groups. The Quakers had a sufficient number of members by 1739 to build their Meeting House, which was situated just to the east of Broad Street on what became Hanover Street. The Anglican Church, St. Michael's, while not the first in Hunterdon County, dates its establishment to circa 1747, and still occupies the original property on Warren Street. (The first Anglican church had been established in 1703 at Hopewell with a second small Anglican group formed at Maidenhead in 1704.)

But the largest religious group in the Trenton area throughout the colonial period was the Presbyterians. They were in the second wave of immigration to the Trenton area which had come from Long Island after 1692, settling principally in Lawrence and Hopewell townships, and they dramatically changed the religious texture of the Trenton area. By 1745, only 3 percent of Hunterdon County residents were Quakers, whereas adjacent Burlington County could claim over 50 percent of the white population as Quakers. The Hopewell and Maidenhead groups were forerunners of the Presbyterians who built the circa-1726 church on East State Street. In addition, both the Presbyterians and the Anglicans sponsored lotteries to raise money to complete and improve their church buildings in 1751 and in 1773. This form of fund-raising was also used by "some

of the principal families in and about Trenton" to build "an English and Grammar School," and, according to an advertisement in the *Pennsylvania Gazette,* to pay "a master to teach such children whose parents are unable to pay for schooling." The schoolhouse was built on a corner of the Presbyterian Meeting House lot on State Street. The school continued in existence through at least the winter of 1780.

The Trenton Mills, located on the south bank of the Assunpink adjacent to the bridge, were the direct successors of Mahlon Stacy's 17th-century gristmill establishment. They were purchased by William Trent, and by 1723 he placed a restriction on all property he sold further upstream forbidding the construction of corn mills, gristmills, fulling mills, or sawmills, thus eliminating competition.

When Trent's mill complex was sold in 1729, the deed described it as:

ye water Grist Mill or Mills being three grist mills under one Roof commonly called . . . Trent's Mills . . . and one fulling Mill . . . and one saw mill or such part as remaineth there of and all boultings Mills set up and Erected in ye mill house of the said Grist Mills.

Joseph Peace, a Trenton resident from 1719 until his death in 1744, actually operated the mills for Trent and a succession of owners. The mills were sold to yet another wealthy Philadelphia merchant, Robert Waln, by owner Robert Lettis Hooper in about 1765. Waln's local supervisor was his nephew, Jesse Waln, who moved to Nottingham Township and built a four-story brick residence at the corner of Ferry Lane and Broad Street. (The residence is now the Eagle Tavern historic restoration.)

Also along the Assunpink were the ironworks established by William Trent, John Porterfield, and Thomas Lambert about 1723, located one mile east of Broad Street on the creek's north bank. The works, which probably manufactured bar iron, incurred severe flood damage to its dam in 1733.

Lots located west of Warren Street, along Pettit's Run, were sold by the Trent family to Isaac Harrow, an English smith, for his steelworks in 1731. His earliest known advertisement appeared in the *American Weekly Mercury,* March 1733, and contained an extensive list of articles, from cowbells to smoothing irons, for sale in both Trenton and Philadelphia. A census of all mills for rolling iron or making steel in the American colonies was ordered in 1750 after the British Parliament forbade the construction of any additional forges or furnaces. The sheriff of Hunterdon County reported that Harrow's plating mill and furnace, then owned by Benjamin Yard, were the only known ones in the county. Steel was produced in Trenton and advertised for sale in New York and Philadelphia newspapers by several owners and tenants of the works up to the Hessian occupation of Trenton in 1776.

The third major processing industry in the Trenton area was the tanning of leather, which dated back to the early years of the 18th century. Of four such establishments known to be in operation in Trenton, the oldest and largest was that of Stacy Potts on the upper west side of Warren Street just below Bank Street.

But it was the presence of a dependable ferry at the Falls that made a remarkable difference in the rural nature of the Trenton area. James Trent received a patent from the royal governor to operate a ferry that would permit the convenient passage of travellers, horses, and freight. He established it below the Falls, a little south of Bloomsbury Court, and laid out Ferry Street to direct traffic from the main road, South Broad Street. By 1770 Trenton had succeeded in capturing the major share of the traffic between New York and Philadelphia, according to John Pomfret's *Colonial New Jersey.*

An intensive rivalry developed when a new ferry was established by Elijah Bond south of Trent's ferry crossing in the 1770s. The location offered an advantage because the ferry was further removed from the Falls' turbulence and the crowding of the shallop (boat) landings there. But the older ferry continued to dominate the business until early in the 19th century. As it had in the beginning, the river continued to shape the fortune of the town.

Chapter Two

A "PRETTY VILLAGE" IN THE MIDST OF WAR

On the morning of December 26, 1776, in spite of heavy snow and high winds, Washington's forces attacked the Hessian garrison at Trenton. Within an hour the American Army won a sweeping victory. This lithograph by Heppenheimer and Maurer appeared in the Centennial Album in 1875.

The famous American statesman John Adams observed the Trenton area as he rode south from Princeton on an August day in 1774. Stopping to breakfast at Williams' Tavern at the Trenton ferry, Adams garnered a favorable impression of the countryside and noted in his diary that Trenton was "a pretty village." "It appears to be the largest town we have seen in the Jerseys," he wrote. Other visitors echoed his impressions. During the following winter months, another visitor, Robert Honyman, recorded in *Colonial Panorama, 1775* this impression of the area:

The Delaware, where we cross it here is about a quarter of a mile broad, and two miles further is Trenton in Jersey Colony. Stopt here and dined. Trenton is a pretty little town and most beautiful fields to the Northwest sloping down to the river Delaware. From Trenton to Princeton is 12 miles, the roads at present excessive bad.

Trenton's river location, which drew travellers like Adams and Honyman, would continue to play a dominant role in the area's history throughout the Revolutionary War period. Here battles would be fought; armies would encamp; congresses and legislatures would compete for housing and meeting space; and historic river crossings would be immortalized by artists and historians.

The war came quickly, and then remained for eight years to disrupt the lives of those who had chosen to settle near the Falls of the Delaware.

As Trentonians gathered on Monday, July 8, 1776 to hear the stirring and rebellious words of the Declaration of Independence read publicly from their courthouse, the state's soldiers were campaigning in locales as far away as Canada. Five months later, the town's inhabitants would have their lives, their fortunes, and their virtue held in jeopardy as Hessian soldiers occupied the Trenton area in the winter of that year.

Trentonians had endured several episodes with military forces in their midst during the closing decades of the colonial period, and, as a community, were not known for their hospitality toward soldiers. During the French and Indian War, British mercenary troops had been sent to America to protect the colonists from Indian attack, especially along the upper Delaware River. About 250 of them arrived in Trenton in December 1756, and were quartered for the winter in residents' houses. The householders complained bitterly and filed petitions with the powerless Jersey Legislature. Relief was to come briefly in the following April when the unwanted boarders left for the Halifax expedition. But in September, 600 sick soldiers were sent back to New Jersey for billeting and for nursing care in private homes. When additional soldiers arrived later in the fall of 1757, conditions in Trenton became more intolerable than in the preceding winter. The aroused and angry citizens of Trenton proposed to the colonial assembly (the lower legislative house) that they be allowed to "speedily . . . erect and build such sufficient and convenient barracks" as would prevent such conditions from recurring.

In May 1758, the barracks construction was begun on a lot about an acre in size on the northern edge of the town, close to the river. The barracks, which was made of local stone, housed about 300 soldiers who arrived the following December and stayed every winter through 1763. When Parliament, with the hated Stamp Act of 1765, provided for the permanent quartering of British troops in America at the expense of the colonies, the Royal Governor of New Jersey, William Franklin, and the assembly regularly quarreled over appropriations to supply the five barracks in the colony—with the assemblymen voicing the popular resentment against raising taxes to maintain an army in peacetime. In April 1771, the Freeholders in Hunterdon County, who had a close-up view of the goings-on at the Trenton barracks, instructed their assemblymen to consider the vice and immorality spread throughout the community and the danger to civil establishment when troops were quartered among the general population. The experience in Trenton (and other areas) with "quartering large bodies of armed troops among" civilians and keeping "standing armies without the consent of our legislatures" was angrily denounced by Thomas Jefferson and was one of the causes of the Declaration of Independence.

On the eve of revolution, with a population of about 500 people concentrated in the vicinity of Trent's triangle of Broad, Warren, and Front streets, Trenton was already an embryonic city. By 1774 there were four identifiable and interacting elements operating to fuse the falls area into a city: a population that came together as a community to promote the public welfare; a topography that not only permitted growth but actually encouraged it; a varied economic base of craftsmen and industries; and social organizations that created cultural activities. In 1774 the colony of New Jersey had a

population of about 120,000; the small number of Trenton residents was deceiving for it served as a magnet community for the rural region surrounding the falls. Basically, the royal borough of Trenton continued to exist in the minds of the people, even though politically they were situated in two counties, and four townships.

Religious tolerance was evident in the town, which had by this time four Protestant communities: Presbyterian, Anglican, Quaker, and, most recently, Methodist. There was a permanent structure for the town's school and a cooperative system that administered it. Regular stage service to New York (via what was commonly termed the "flying machine") connected with ferry crossings to Pennsylvania and promoted the business of servicing travellers. (By 1771, the stage line's goal was to reduce the running time between Philadelphia and New York City to one and a half days, but the journey usually took most of two days.) There was a postmaster, Abraham Hunt, who served both before and after the war, and, according to a Philadelphia newspaper, "an elegant public library" that had been founded in 1750. The Trenton Library Company began with a £500 donation from Dr. Thomas Cadwalader, a chief burgess of the royal borough of Trenton.

Outside of Trenton, the region was obviously rural. South of the Assunpink Creek were several small Burlington County settlements such as Kingsbury, Trenton Ferry, and Lamberton, that nourished Trenton's economy. Many of these hamlets' inhabitants engaged in milling operations along the Assunpink's south bank, or in fish pickling or transporting goods and people. The set-

Above: To guard New Jersey from attack by the French and their Indian allies, five military barracks were built at strategic points throughout the colony. In Trenton, soldiers' quarters were built on a central courtyard in 1758, and officers' quarters were added later. In 1776 part of the Hessian garrison was lodged here. William E. Pedrick's painting depicts a line of infantry on parade leaving the Trenton barracks. Courtesy, The Old Barracks Museum

Facing page: A fascinating view of Trenton on the eve of the first battle is conveyed in this engraving by F. Humphrys (after a painting by James Hamilton). The rural atmosphere of the "pretty village" is evident. The scene was painted for Godey's Magazine and was printed circa 1860 by W.S. Winship. Courtesy, New Jersey State Museum (NJSM)

tlers lived in modest frame homes for the most part, although a few had large estate homes like the Trent House of Dr. William Bryant. Lamberton, whose only industry was Lambert's tanyards, was largely rural until the 1750s when a fishery was established. This marked Lamberton's transition to a storage and wharfing district to serve the sloops that plied the lower Delaware, although the town remained primarily an adjunct to Trenton.

Most of the township of Trenton was rural as were the neighboring Hopewell, Maidenhead, and Nottingham townships. Stephanie Smith Toothman's analytical work on Trenton Township shows that in 1779, 47 out of 61 farmers owned over 100 acres each. More than two-thirds of those had inherited the bulk of their property, and were the second generation of colonists. Although many had made considerable progress in clearing and fencing fields, so that the influence of one generation of European settlers was apparent in the landscape, Toothman's study concludes that only slightly more than half of the lots had been cleared by the 1770s. Thus travellers would see substantial tracts of virgin forests as well as attractive farmlands and compact hamlets as they passed, for example, through the 129 major land holdings in Maidenhead Township.

Generally, the residents of the area did not follow the European custom of primogeniture, whereby the eldest son or male relative inherited the father's entire estate. Most men divided their property among their sons and, in the case of Quakers, also made some provisions for

their daughters' financial security. Thus the average size of the individual farm declined significantly between 1703 and the onset of the Revolutionary War, by which time it had become about 50 acres in some areas.

The citizenry of Trenton Township, by the time of the Revolution, was made up of a mixture of country gentlemen, businessmen, and craftsmen. Many persons pursued several trades. Francis Witt advertised in 1782 that he kept "a house of entertainment for man and horse, at the sign of Alexander the Great" at Trenton Ferry, where he also had a hairdressing partnership for ladies and gentlemen and sold hairpins, powder, and pomade; he also offered a small house to rent. Among the varied services available, according to newspaper notices, were those of two hosiers, two tailors, two staymakers, two hatters, one shoemaker, one gold-and-silversmith, one gunsmith, one clock- and watchmaker, three blacksmiths, one medical doctor, one druggist, one tobacconist, one hairdresser, several lawyers, and a

printer who was also a bookbinder and bookseller.

Most of the nine general stores in the town were located along North Warren Street. One such storekeeper, Joseph Milnor, publicly advertised in September 1781 that he had "a few of the newest fashioned Windsor Chairs" to supplement his usual stock of wines, rum, sugar, teas, coffee, spices, copper teakettles, chisels, boards and shingles, hollowware, padlocks, window glass, and assorted dry goods. Another store, in the *New Jersey Gazette* of July 4, 1781, offered a variety of merchandise and "a healthy negro wench 24 years old, and a boy 18, sold for want of employ only."

The village came close to destruction even before the British and American armies fought over it. On January 30, 1772, fire destroyed six structures and seriously damaged more than seven others along Warren between State and Hanover streets. Water to extinguish the fire was supplied by personal garden wells (the town's only water source), and the cold, windy winter made chimney sparks a continuing hazard even in a town where most of the houses (usually made of wood) were separated by a side garden. The 1772 fire no doubt stimulated the formation of the volunteer group, the Hand-in-Hand Fire Company, in April of that year. The city's two fire companies, the Union (organized in 1747) and the Hand-in-Hand, kept their engines near the town center along Warren Street, and drew their membership from all the prominent men of the area. An observer at the 1772 fire was reported to have said, "I believe, for a considerable time we expected nearly the whole town to have been destroyed." War would bring that danger again to Trenton.

The initial skirmishes of the American Revolution were far distant and involved people and issues that seemed to have no effect on the lives of Trentonians. Today it may be difficult to imagine the days when the war of independence was beginning and there was not even one newspaper published in New Jersey. Some regional news was obtained by citizens who subscribed to the post rider delivery of one of the seven Pennsylvania or four New York weekly papers.

But Trenton was more fortunate than many New Jersey communities for current news was received from the continuous stream of travellers who, while passing through the community, reinforced the social and political role played by the town's several taverns. In December 1777 the New Jersey state government subsidized Quaker Isaac Collins in publishing the *New Jersey*

These are the times that try men's souls. The summer soldier and the sunshine patriot will, in this crisis, shrink from the service of their country.

These lines appeared in *The Crisis*, a popular pamphlet, as the American Army retreated from the Hudson to the Delaware River banks; and it was those words that Washington would order read aloud to the raggedly clothed soldiers of his army. They would hear those words on Christmas day, 1776, as they grouped for an attack in weather that was "fearfully cold and raw," with "a snowstorm setting in," as Captain Thomas Forrest wrote.

It must have been a cold, raw time for the citizens of the Trenton area too. The British Army was in control of the state and 1,586 of their mercenaries—Hessian officers and enlisted men—were lodged in winter quarters in the town. Daily troop patrols and six picket posts

Above left: Against intense cold and blizzard winds, Washington's army made its dramatic crossing of the ice-choked Delaware. Using Durham ore boats and flat-bottomed ferries, the army gained the steep riverbanks and commenced the march on Trenton. This lithograph by Heppenheimer and Maurer appeared in a Centennial Album in 1875.

Facing page top: As a commander of the New Jersey militia, Brigadier General Philemon Dickinson paved the way for Washington's victory with attacks against the Hessian garrison in Trenton. The pressure of sudden raids and skirmishes left the Hessian force nervous and weary. In later years

Dickinson returned to his Trenton mansion, "The Hermitage," and continued to be a prominent leader in the civic life of the town. (NJSL)

Facing page bottom: An American division commenced artillery fire at 8:00 a.m. on December 26, 1776, from the high ground north of the town. Under Washington were officers such as Nathanael Greene, Henry Knox, and Alexander Hamilton. Lieutenant James Monroe, only 18, was one of the few Americans wounded in the action. This painting, by William Pedrick, shows the Warren Street houses with shutters closed against the snow. Courtesy, The Old Barracks Museum

Gazette. The paper was originally printed at Burlington, but in little more than a year Collins decided that Trenton was a more central location for his weekly newspaper. On March 4, 1778 Collins published Trenton's first paper, which he continued publishing through the war years until November 27, 1786. Collins' printing office attracted another new business to Trenton, a paper mill, which was established in December 1778 to supply that scarce product. Collins, himself official printer for the state government's proceedings and laws, sought and won legislative support to promote a local mill. Stacy Potts, local businessman and later mayor of Trenton, joined with the experienced Germantown papermaker, John Reynolds, to announce in Collins' *New Jersey Gazette* that their Trenton mill was nearly complete. They were successful and produced paper for two years, from the spring of 1779 through the winter of 1781.

Although the Revolutionary War's military confrontations started in Massachusetts, it was in the small New Jersey region between New York and Philadelphia that General Washington's army would spend at least one-quarter of the war years. Under conditions of retreat, victory, or watchful waiting, Washington travelled the roads of the Trenton area. The 1776-1777 winter campaign of Washington from Trenton to Princeton has been described by contemporary military historians as the ten most crucial days of the war. In New Jersey during those battle-filled days in early December 1776, Thomas Paine penned the words:

guarding the major roadways reminded them of the retreating American Army and their own depressed hopes for independence. The air was filled with the gossip of British depredations and Hessian rapes.

The account of the crossing of the Delaware is a dramatic one. In the middle of a snowstorm, with a sharp frost, a river current difficult to pass, ice increasing in the main channel and a high wind, Colonel John Glover and his Marblehead sailors transported the Americans over to the New Jersey shore in the shallow draft Durham boats. Artillery and horses moved across the Delaware via several ferries since the Durham boats were not wide enough to handle them. Meanwhile, the commander of

the Hessian forces, Colonel Johann Gottlieb Rall, was enjoying the hospitality of Trenton's leading merchant, Abraham Hunt. The entertainment took the form of a cards-and-wine party and although it continued late into the night, it was not the drunken, carousing Christmas celebration it was previously thought to be. The troops, devout Lutherans, honored Christmas as a holy day and probably would not have been in the custom of drinking to excess to celebrate it. Rall, however, could easily have been enjoying a pleasant social gathering after months of Spartan conditions while persuing the American Army. This would have explained his refusal to interview personally a man who interrupted the evening by searching Rall out at Hunt's house. When Hunt's Negro servant refused to disturb the party by admitting the Loyalist spy, the latter put his information in a note. Rall, when given the note, thrust it into his pocket without reading it—an inconceivable folly for a soldier.

Military historian Kemble Widmer states in his booklet, *The Christmas Campaign*:

By Christmas day, as a result of [their] "du jour" rotation and other duties, many of the Hessians were so tired as to be hardly fit for duty.

The soldiers were on five-minute calls, fully uniformed for 24-hour periods once every three days while being quartered in the alarm houses (du jour duty). Militia harassment, added to the Hessian fear of an attack from the unconventional Americans, had Rall's three regiments out on numerous patrols and reinforced sentry duties. And yet Washington surprised them and defeated them.

The explanation could very well be the presence of Brigadier-General Philemon Dickinson, originally the Colonel of the Hunterdon County militia and at the time of the battle commander of the First Brigade of the New Jersey Militia, encamped near Yardley, Pennsylvania. Dickinson had purchased "the Hermitage" (part of which still sits facing the river on Colonial Avenue). Rall had placed a detachment of his Jaegers, who were expert marksmen, in the Hermitage. The 50 soldiers destroyed the greenhouse, made a bonfire with a choice Chippendale chair and other furnishings, covered the lawn with broken decanters, and stabled their horses in the library where they kicked down some of the fireplace tiles. This wanton destruction of an elegant country house was witnessed by its owner through a spyglass from his Pennsylvania headquarters at Yardley's Farm. But Dickinson didn't just sit quietly; he led Jersey militia units across the Delaware (probably using Yardley's-Howell's ferry) to harass and raid enemy positions on the militia's own terrain. Local Hunterdon and Burlington County men, who had taken up arms in defense of American independence, now skirmished with foreign troops who were occupying their homes and frightening

Above: This illustration from Ballou's Pictorial Drawing Room Companion, which appeared in 1855, shows the corner of Warren and Greene streets and Pennington Road where the American artillery opened fire at the First Battle of Trenton on December 26, 1776. In 1893 the Battle Monument was erected to mark this historic site. Courtesy, The New Jersey Historical Society (NJHS)

Facing page: Washington is shown at the First Battle of Trenton in an engraving by William and Thomas Illman after a painting by Edward Lamson Henry. The view is typical of 19th-century patriotic versions of the battle. Washington did not ride between the lines of fire at Trenton (although he did so at Princeton a few days later), and the hats and swords worn by the soldiers are inaccurate for the period. (NJSM)

their families into flight. General Dickinson's scouting parties killed a patrolling light dragoon in Pennington on December 17. The next day, Dickinson landed a small detachment four miles north of Trenton, and in the ensuing skirmish killed one of the Jaegers sent to investigate from their post at the Hermitage. On the 19th, Rall suffered additional losses when a Dickinson scouting party captured three men of the Von Lossberg regiment who had gone out to obtain forage two miles from Trenton, not far from the road to Maidenhead.

Military historian Samuel Steele Smith has compiled evidence of the initiative and bravery of Dickinson's Jersey militia, who crossed the river daily to harass the Hessians in organized fashion. Their activities contributed greatly to the success of Washington's main attack on Trenton. Dickinson's local troops used guerilla tactics, especially sniping, to control the area near Howell's ferry on the New Jersey side of the river, and thus the Hessians were never able to use the ferries further north (McKonkey's-Johnson's), so that Washington could use them to make his famous night crossing when he resolved to take Trenton.

Having crossed the Delaware by four in the morning on December 26, Washington's 2,388 men were placed in two divisions. The first, commanded by General John Sullivan, approached Trenton by the river road, while

the second, commanded by General Nathanael Greene, advanced along the Pennington Road. They reached the town by eight o'clock, after marching for eight miles through a blizzard, and as Greene's division opened artillery and musket fire at the junction of Broad and Warren streets, Sullivan's men attacked from the river road. Caught between the American forces, the three Hessian regiments, after an hour's resistance, surrendered. Over 900 Hessians were captured and were marched away as Washington withdrew his victorious army and recrossed the river.

There are many accounts of the military actions during those ten crucial days but few civilian commentaries on the terror endured by the common citizen desperate to maintain a normal rhythm of living. Fiery patriots were few; so were the dedicated Loyalists who would permanently leave for a new home in England. We can read between the lines of surviving documents and newspapers that the mood of the general population was fear and resentment that they were thrust into the midst of contending armies and political ideologies. However, one civilian account specifically noted that on December 11 a group of American soldiers on the Pennsylvania side of the Delaware saw a number of women on the opposite shore calling for help, and when they went over in the boats to assist them, they discovered that all the

women had been abused by the enemy troops, and that one, a girl about fifteen years old, had been raped that morning by a British officer. In another account Stacy Potts' grandson, Stacy G., in his manuscript *Autobiography,* (1859) noted two civilian casualties. He wrote that his grandfather's frame house near the corner of Warren and Bank streets (one of the best in Trenton) "was a good deal riddled by the American cannonade directed down Warren Street at the commencement of the battle." Daughter Betsy, about 11 years old, had been staying all night with a sick lady, Miss Coxe, who lived nearby. Terror-stricken as the fighting began, Betsy ran homeward down the street and was wounded in the head by a musket ball. The rest of the family hid in the cellar but that did not prevent a fatality. Betsy's uncle (brother of her mother, Margaret Yardley), was killed by a musket ball that entered his room. In Washington's own dispatch to the Continental Congress (then in Baltimore), he wrote, "our loss is very trifling indeed— only two officers and one or two privates wounded." Washington made no mention of the effect his soldiers had on the confused, frightened civilian inhabitants when such fighting occurs in the streets of a small town.

Stacy Potts carried on the tannery business very successfully, and later served as mayor of Trenton, but during the war his house was frequently used as officers'

quarters for both armies. His grandson stated that some 19th-century historians had said that Potts kept a tavern, but he dismissed this as "a conceit at which the old gentleman would probably have been much amused, if it had been coined or announced in his lifetime" (1731-1816), for he married three times and had at least seven children in his home during the war years. His grandson said the fact was, that as a Quaker in a country at war, he entertained the friends of his country by choice, her enemies by compulsion. Colonel Rall, the commander of the Hessians, was quartered at the Potts home, and having been mortally wounded in the battle of December 26th, was brought back to the Potts home and died the next day. General Washington and Greene visited the dying man after the battle, and Stacy Potts, who was present, said the former shed tears on bidding Rall farewell. Betsy Potts, with her head bandaged, helped tend the mortally wounded Rall, who was buried in an unmarked grave in the Presbyterian Church yard.

Another Trentonian called upon to care for the wounded after the First Battle of Trenton was the resident of the Trent House, Dr. William Bryant. Historians ascribe Loyalist sympathy to him but he continued his practice of medicine and rendered services to wounded Americans throughout the war. Bryant had been noticeably friendly with the Hessians, but it should be remembered he had a detachment of 30 Hessian infantrymen stationed in his house to support the guard at the Trenton Ferry. A man of scholarly tastes, Bryant was elected to the elite American Philosophical Society in 1774. His later close association with Dr. Nicholas de Belleville, a French physician who came to this country in the entourage of Count Casimer Pulaski, was strong enough to convince the Frenchman to settle in Trenton. This would seem to discount the belief that Bryant had

been a committed Loyalist. It seems more probable that, like Stacy Potts, he was a realist—well respected throughout the community for his medical abilities and scholarly reputation—who tried to stay away from politics while protecting his wealth. When he died in 1786 at Bloomsbury, his inventory included several Negro slaves.

Other residents were more committed to the British cause. One woman, Mrs. Brereton (Mary) Pointing, guided the British to the house of John Abbott in rural Nottingham the day after they occupied the area. With General Howe approaching Trenton in early December 1776, the state treasurer, Samuel Tucker of Hunterdon County, placed about £6,000 in Jersey paper money and various important public documents in a chest which was hidden in the Abbott house five miles east of Trenton. His plan was known to Mary Pointing who promptly had the house searched by British troops.

During the battle of Trenton on December 26, Colonel John Cadwalader had been unable to cross his artillery for a coordinated attack downriver in the Burlington area, but was finally able to cross his entire force the next day. Cautiously surrounding Burlington, he learned that the Hessians had withdrawn to Crosswicks, then Allentown, and finally to Princeton on December 28 after the news of the Trenton battle had reached them. Cadwalader then proceeded northward to Bordentown with his force of 1,600. Washington crossed back to Trenton on December 30, and ordered Cadwalader to continue his northward march to join the main army as quickly as possible. This would bring a force of approximately 7,000 Americans against 10,000 British under Cornwallis who were moving to counteract the American victory at Trenton.

Washington chose a native of Trenton, Colonel Joseph Reed, to lead a foray into Princeton to gather intelligence about the British headquarters there. Reed had graduated from the College of New Jersey (Princeton) and had practiced law in Trenton before the war. He took 12 men of the Philadelphia Troop of Cavalry with him on Quaker Road to within three miles of Princeton. Riding around Princeton, the scouting party captured 12 dragoons at Wilson's farmhouse. The British soldiers had been requisitioning corn for their horses, and had relaxed their guard while in Mrs. Wilson's kitchen, as one resident described it, "conquering a parcel of mince pyes." Reed had one of the captives mounted behind each member of his party and thus

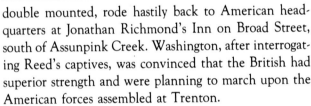

double mounted, rode hastily back to American headquarters at Jonathan Richmond's Inn on Broad Street, south of Assunpink Creek. Washington, after interrogating Reed's captives, was convinced that the British had superior strength and were planning to march upon the American forces assembled at Trenton.

Writing in the 1970s, local military historians Samuel Steele Smith and Kemble Widmer provide exact details of the action-filled days surrounding the battle of the Assunpink (or the Second Battle of Trenton). For those who called this area home, the severe weather was exacerbated by the scarce supply of food and firewood caused by the commandeering by the military of both sides. Trenton, which had been devoid of any military presence except for a few severely wounded Hessians, enjoyed the respite for only three days when the American troops descended upon them. One can imagine the consternation of the local citizens—unhappy when 300 soldiers were quartered at the Barracks—at having to host 7,000 battle-worn soldiers. The number of men was so great that they were quartered not only in houses throughout the town but in the outskirts as far out as Philemon Dickinson's home, which was over a mile north of town.

The first day of the new year found American forces assigned to the small village of Lawrenceville. Washington meant this to be a rearguard operation, where, by utilizing every natural obstacle, the British would be forced to deploy, at least once, thinking that this operation was the major confrontation.

As the main British army passed through Lawrenceville at about noon on January 2, they encountered an American picket which shot a mounted Hessian from his horse. The picket retired with a small advance party from the Little Shabakunk to the more southern Shabakunk Creek, where the main American position was held, under the command of a Pennsylvanian, Colonel Edward Hand. The Americans then pulled down the wooden bridge that traversed the Shabakunk, and took up advantageous positions in the nearby mile-thick woods on the south side of the creek which faced, across a difficult ford, open fields to be crossed by the British on their march. The fire from the Pennsylvania rifles was so deadly that the enemy halted until their artillery could be brought up to scour the woods for half an hour. It was during this cannonade that Generals Greene, Knox, and Washington rode out to the Shabakunk to encourage the men. Washington told Colonel Hand that it was important to retard the British march to Trenton until nightfall. Hand's skirmish at the creek consumed two hours before he was compelled to retreat to his next line of defense. One battalion headed down the Lawrenceville Road and a Virginia brigade followed along closer to the Assunpink to keep from being outflanked by the determined British march. At Philip's Mill on the Assunpink, rifle shots were exchanged with some Hessian cannon shots, but the American defense was so fierce that a Hessian battalion and the remainder of the

Rall brigade were left there to prevent an American attack on the flank of the British march from Lawrenceville to Trenton.

At a ravine known as Stockton Hollow, which crossed Princeton Avenue, the Americans placed two cannons in a commanding position over the approach into Trenton. Here effective fire upon the British columns for almost half an hour caused them to bring up their artillery for a counter-barrage. It also forced the main British effort off the roads and further north, with firing from the musket muzzles visible to the Americans in the sunset dusk. Meanwhile, the pressure of the larger British forces had the defensive Americans marching down Broad Street under cover of American artillery stationed between the south side of Assunpink Creek and the Delaware River. Washington was at the creek as the men crossed over the narrow bridge—a dense mass with the enemy harassing their rear. The last Americans, covering the final retreat, were forced into the water and reached the safe southern bank although their colonel was captured in the final moments.

British Light Infantry tried first to take the bridge, though unsuccessfully; then a heavy column of Hessian grenadiers made an assault, supported by two cannons firing from Broad Street. There were also two hidden behind "Mr. Waln's house opposite the Mill and some Riflemen in the Mill, and artillery all along the creek." An intense cannonade exchange from a range of less than 500 yards, and in the dark, was costly to both sides but the American gunners were successful in repulsing the British-Hessian attack. Although the artillery firing stopped at about seven o'clock, the Americans occasionally sent over a few shots to keep the enemy away from the creek. It was a successful strategy because the attackers withdrew about one and a half miles to bivouac in the woods south of the Shabakunk. The mild and pleasant weather of the day gave way to an intensely cold freezing night, making the river once again impassable to boats.

Washington, having conferred with his officers in the house of Alexander Douglass, decided to leave Trenton before the British could attack and trap his army against

Facing page: Washington summoned his officers to a conference in the house of Alexander Douglass on the evening of January 2, 1777. It was here that they decided to leave the British army behind and march north during the night to Princeton. In William Pedrick's painting the individual officers from left to right are: Sullivan, Greene, Cadwalader, Mercer, Ewing, St. Clair, Washington, Dickinson, Reed, Hand, Stark, Mifflin, Stephens, and Knox. Courtesy, The Old Barracks Museum

Above: The house of Alexander Douglass, then on South Broad (Queen) Street, was Brigadier General St. Clair's headquarters during the Second Battle of Trenton. Washington held a council of his officers here on the evening of January 2, 1777, which led to the night march to Princeton. The house has been moved and now stands at Front and Montgomery streets on the edge of Mill Hill Park. (NJSM)

the river. Accordingly, the American forces departed on the Sandtown Road (Hamilton Avenue), leaving behind their campfires to deceive Cornwallis. Early the next morning, January 3, Washington defeated and captured a detachment of 1,000 British at the battle of Princeton. Among the casualties was his friend and fellow Virginian General Hugh Mercer who fell mortally wounded. With Cornwallis leading the British army from Trenton in pursuit, Washington marched north and withdrew to winter quarters in Morristown. In ten days his army had won three victories, taken 2,000 prisoners, and permanently altered the course of the Revolutionary War.

In 1781 Trentonians witnessed another confrontation: the dramatic and peaceful conclusion of the most serious mutiny in the Continental Army. The events are described in Carl Van Doren's Mutiny in January. The soldiers of the Pennsylvania Line had served for several years continuously, had suffered intense cold and hunger, were without sufficient clothing, blankets, and medicine, and had not been paid for two years. On January 1, 1781 at the Jockey Hollow encampment in New Jersey, 1,700 angry men mutinied; in disciplined ranks commanded by 12 regimental sergeants, and hauling four artillery pieces, they began their march south to demand justice from Congress. Steadily they advanced past Pluckemin, Somerville, and Rocky Hill to Princeton. There they camped while holding initial negotiations with Trentonian Joseph Reed, who represented Congress.

Dissatisfied with these discussions, the troops and their accompanying women marched for five hours on January 9 to Trenton, where they advanced down Broad Street to Ferry Street and turned into a field beside the Delaware to pitch their tents. General Anthony Wayne was the active field commander of the Pennsylvania Line. His men, who respected him, declared their intention to fight for him in spite of the mutiny, if the British approached. General Wayne and Joseph Reed were guests of Colonel John Cox in the Trent House, while the regimental sergeants stayed at Jonathan Richmond's Tavern. The official negotiations lasted for two weeks. After the mutineers were persuaded to give up the four heavy guns, each man received 50 shillings, rations for travel, and a discharge. About two-thirds of them re-enlisted, were given a bounty and leave, and later returned to duty. They then departed from Trenton, where they had behaved well, and on January 29, Wayne reported to Washington that the mutiny was over.

In October 1781 the streets of Trenton were again filled with the sound of marching, and many soldiers camped overnight in the river meadows below the Eagle Tavern as the Americans, under Washington, and the French, under General Rochambeau, swept south to surround a major British army at Yorktown, Virginia.

Again Cornwallis would confront Washington and again the Americans would emerge victorious. Cornwallis is reputed to have told Washington that history would count his brightest victory as having been won "on the banks of the Delaware" rather than on the banks of the Chesapeake, a reference to the surrender on the Virginia peninsula jutting into Chesapeake Bay. For Trentonians, victory meant a return to the business of living, and a renewed sense of purpose for the "pretty village" on the banks of the Delaware.

Chapter Three

A CAPITAL PLACE

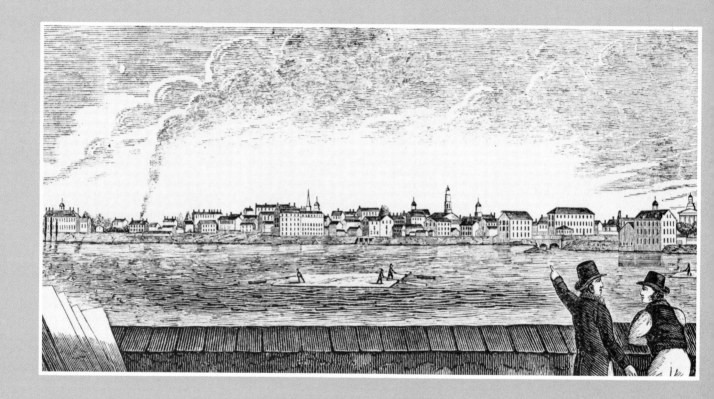

This view of Trenton, from a history of
New Jersey by John Barber and Henry
Howe (printed in 1846), shows the state
capital as a river port of churches, public
buildings, and mills. Several towers are
visible where factory chimneys would
later stand. The State House can be seen
on the extreme left and the Mercer
County Courthouse on the far right.
Courtesy, Early Woodcut Views of
New York and New Jersey, Dover

The Trenton area received the news of Lord Cornwallis' surrender with a public celebration of joy one week after the event on Saturday, October 27, 1781. Officials from Trenton and the adjacent townships cooperated with state officials in quickly organizing a festive, well-ordered day of activities that started with a special service at the Presbyterian Church conducted by the Reverend Elihu Spencer. At noon a cannonade was fired by the town's corps of artillery. The *New Jersey Gazette* reported that General Philemon Dickinson, with gentlemen from the town and neighborhood, joined Governor William Livingston and the state legislators on the town common. After an elegant entertainment at John Cape's tavern, the French Arms, where 13 toasts were drunk, the day's festivities concluded with "a brilliant illumination" at seven that evening.

To commemorate the birth of the French dauphin, a similar public celebration occurred in Trenton. Also held in the French Arms, it was attended by Governor Livingston and the members of the State Council and Assembly, in addition to the prominent men of the Trenton vicinity, on May 24, 1782. The Treaty of Paris in 1783 also occasioned events planned cooperatively between the inhabitants of Trenton and New Jersey officials, this time involving entertainments in at least three taverns along Warren Street.

The cooperative and patriotic attitude displayed by the community leaders is evidence that they were interested in promoting the status of the area. They believed that Trenton could be more than a village of 1,000 inhabitants which only serviced travelers. Local officials were working for a greater role in the political affairs of the state and of the nation, neither of which had a permanent seat of government.

When the first state legislature was organized in 1776, they met originally in Princeton during the late summer and later moved briefly to Burlington, the colonial capital of West Jersey, before fleeing ahead of enemy troops to Pittstown and Haddonfield. The state officials would have a variety of temporary seats of government while the Jerseys earned the nickname "Cockpit of the Revolution."

However great the relief of Trentonians when Washington swept the occupying British and Hessian troops out of Jersey into New York City, the citizens still did not take kindly to soldiers being stationed in their midst, even Americans. On the first anniversary of the Second Battle of Trenton, for example, four local magistrates

Early in his career, William Livingston's Presbyterian principles inclined him toward political independence. He served as the first state governor from 1776 to 1790 during the crisis years of the revolution. On April 16, 1783, he read a preliminary peace proclamation to a large crowd at Trenton. A local committee replied: "We recollect with pleasure and veneration, that when the helm of state was committed to your hands . . . you accepted with firmness the perilous station. . . ." Courtesy, State of New Jersey

(William Cleayton, Benjamin Yard, Rensselaer Williams, and Benjamin Van Cleave) appealed directly to General Washington to prevent four regiments of light dragoons from wintering in Trenton. They cited the danger of the presence of troops, which, they felt, would encourage the British army to make an incursion into their neighborhood, threatening to make their streets again a battlefield. The town, according to the magistrates, was "so much a Thoroughfare, that many teams as well as travellers in the public employ necessarily depend on finding temporary supplies" and lodgings to continue their journey. As established in the early decades of the 18th century, and followed by the 19th century's railroads, the main north-south route from

New England to the southern states crossed the Delaware at Trenton.

The magistrates' document went on to state: "The county for ten miles round and upwards being so much exhausted, that although the horses and cattle within that circumference are far less numerous than usual, the forage remaining will afford them a very scanty subsistence for the winter."

The state legislature was also brought into the town's petition since it was scheduled to convene in the town early in February (February 11 to April 4, 1778). Only with great difficulty could accommodations be made for the men and their horses, and yet, the magistrates continued to argue, there was not another town in the state equally remote from the enemy (which held both New York City and Philadelphia) that was in any better condition to provide for so many. The inconvenience of the previous session in Princeton had caused the legislators to leave several important state matters unfinished; so, the Trenton magistrates wrote, the urgent needs of civil government should be considered more important than the need to find winter quarters for American troops.

Lastly, the argument mentioned the damage caused by

The old Masonic Hall, built in 1793, was a meeting place for many prominent Trenton citizens during the 19th century. Now maintained as a museum, the hall housed the first free school in New Jersey which opened in 1833.

the two battles previously fought in Trenton, pointing out that Trenton's citizens had "suffered so much injury by the ravages of the enemy, and other events of the war that most has not yet been repaired for want of the proper materials and workmen." A visitor, Ebenezer Hazard, went through central New Jersey in August 1777 and wrote in his diary that the fences all about the Trenton area had been destroyed and that the ferry house was burned down. The January 2, 1778 appeal of the magistrates undoubtedly expressed the feelings of the people of Trenton when it stated, "we have already felt the calamities of war in a degree unknown to most other parts of America."

The damage inflicted on the town's buildings and landscape also added to the strain on the townspeople, who were trying to cope with travellers during four years of very active warfare. This might have been the cause for the removal of the Hunterdon County Seat from Trenton to the Amwell Township home of Henry

Mershon in March 1780. A more likely explanation, however, might be that the war intensified citizens' fear of leaving their family members while they journeyed to the southernmost edge of Hunterdon County to transact even the simplest legal matters such as the filing of wills and deeds. Geography—the distance, poor roads, and poorer maintenance, combined with the almost continuous presence of military forces in the state—as well as township jealousy, are other reasons given by historians for the abandonment of the sandstone courthouse in Trenton. Nonetheless, the building's stucco facade provided an impressive setting for the public proclamations of the news of the war's end on April 15, 1783 and the state's ratification of the new federal constitution on December 19, 1787. The basement jails still held local miscreants—though apparently not very well, as there are numerous notices of escapes in local papers. There must have been a compelling reason for removing the county seat of government from a building which had been especially constructed for county business, and which had been used satisfactorily for 60 years, to a private residence. But the courthouse stood idle, except for the limited number of cases heard by the Admiralty Court, which dealt with maritime matters. And yet the usually vocal Trenton citizenry did not complain too loudly at the loss of the county trade because they were freed to serve the state and national governments.

Considering the description of the times contained in the magistrates' petition, it is not surprising that the state legislature, which met in Trenton for the first sitting of their second session (October 28 to November 1, 1777) was forced to find better accommodations and moved to Princeton for five weeks of business. But their next sitting in Trenton was more pleasant and the legislature came back very frequently.

Given a choice between hosting American soldiers, the Hunterdon County Freeholders, or the state legislators, the town's residents' and leaders' choice reinforced Trenton's decades-old aversion to having military groups quartered in their midst. Perhaps civilians paid better for lodging, or made more purchases from local merchants, but the preferred customers were soon the men who had not yet decided on a state capital. Of the legislative sessions held from 1777 to 1791 (the second to the sixteenth sessions), after which Trenton was made the permanent state capital, the legislature convened 22 times out of 35 in Trenton. Princeton, Burlington, New Brunswick, and Perth Amboy hosted the group several

times but the Trentonians seem to have put together the right combination of meeting space, lodging, and stabling to satisfy the needs of the legislators on a regular basis. Freed from the demands of caring for the county court business, the shrewd business community in Trenton welcomed the more affluent, but peripatetic, state lawmakers. They were so successful that they also hoped and planned to attract the confederation government to the area of the falls.

The appeal of such a clientele might have been the deciding factor in attracting the experienced and capable innkeeper, Jacob G. Bergen, away from Princeton in April 1780. On coming to Trenton he leased the large stone corner house on Warren Street at State. Once the official residence of colonial royal governor Lewis Morris, the property was owned by Samuel Henry, who also operated the iron works on Assunpink Creek. In the early spring of 1780 Henry retired to his farm in Nottingham Township; Bergen then transformed the house by adding an additional story and opening up two rooms on the south side of the first floor main hallway. This created the "Long Room," about 20 by 43 feet in size, with two fireplaces, which was especially suitable for public meetings. The spacious garret was large enough to rent to the State Assembly. This tavern establishment (the French Arms), and Francis Witt's Blazing Star, further north and on the opposite side of Warren Street above State, were the two choice public meeting places in the 1780s.

Other public activities were advertised as occurring in Mrs. Britton's or in Alexander Chambers' house, which probably means their homes were being used as taverns. It was these well-run taverns that attracted the members of the Governor's Council who wrote, in December 1777, that Princeton's "want of convenient and public accommodations must greatly retard the public business, and in proportion augment the public Expense." The council members were not pleased with the changing locations of the legislative meetings since they feared it might give the appearance of instability and wished that the seat of government would be finally established. But it would be 13 years, less a month, before the bill was voted upon in the affirmative in 1790 that fixed the permanent seat of state government at Trenton. In 1791 an act was passed by both houses of the legislature to provide suitable buildings for the accommodation of the legislature and public offices of the state in the newly designated state capital. The bill was not totally unexpected.

Yet it did not prevent other communities such as Princeton, New Brunswick, and Woodbury from maneuvering in the legislature to become the capital or "offering genteel accommodations" in public petitions to the assemblymen and counselors.

Even in the colonial period, Trenton had been a significant enough community to attract the major New Jersey officials, even though the capital alternated between Burlington and Perth Amboy. The citizenry developed almost a tradition of hospitality to governors throughout the 18th century. The first royal governor, Lord Cornbury, attended Whitsunday services at the Anglican Church in Hopewell in 1706. Governor William Cosby and his wife, Grace Montague, stayed several nights in Trenton in late September 1734, on one of his rare excursions into New Jersey, which he ruled along with New York. Lewis Morris, the first royal governor to rule New Jersey as a separate colony from New York, made Trenton his official residence in 1740. First Morris rented the stone stuccoed residence of John Dagworthy at the corner of State and Warren streets. The house faced the County Courthouse and, having been built in the early 1730s, it was the largest and most handsome structure in the town. Perhaps the hubbub of

the court days was not to his liking and so in June 1742 he leased the more rural Trent House, then known as Kingsbury. Morris died there in 1746. Decades would elapse but other governors, not of the colony, but of the state, would have to make their residence in Trenton because of its centralized location, even in so small a state as New Jersey.

When independence became imminent, the New Jersey Committee of Correspondence called upon the state's 13 counties to elect delegates to what is now called the first Provincial Congress. The 85 representatives gathered, not in either of the colonial capitals, but in Trenton. There they remained in session from May to September 1775. The Provincial Congresses, like the subsequent state legislatures, were peripatetic bodies and met at convenient public locations, which in Trenton usually meant one of the several taverns. And so they did through another 15 years of turmoil.

From those years before the state government became a defined place as well as a force, there exists a description of the Trenton scene by a European author. The Marquis de Chastellux's *Travels in North America* recounts his meeting with New Jersey's first governor at a Trenton tavern at Broad and East Hanover streets:

I found my headquarters well established in a fine inn kept by Mr. Rensselaer Williams. . . . I had scarcely alighted from my horse before I received a visit from Mr. William Livingston, Governor of the two Jerseys. He is a much respected old man, and considered a very sensible one. He was pleased to accompany me on a little walk I took before dinner, to reconnoiter the environs of the town and see the camp occupied by the Americans before the affair of Princeton.

The 18th-century translator of Chastellux's account added his own comments about Livingston as a gentleman so active and useful in the revolution that he was long the marked object of Tory vengeance. Livingston was obliged, for many months, to shift his quarters every day, but nothing would abate his zeal; he never quitted his government, and was indefatigable in his exertions— and evidently held in high regard by the French.

Research done by Carlos Godfrey for his history, *The Mechanics National Bank,* uncovers the fact that Governor Livingston did not lodge at one of the taverns in Trenton while conducting the business of the state government, but stayed with the Crolius family. In 1783 Peter Crolius had offered three rooms with fireplaces and daily dining for up to ten people, probably at his

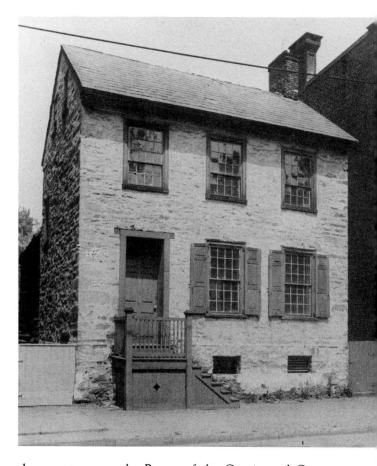

Facing page: Trenton became the permanent state capital in 1790. In 1791 an act passed to provide for state buildings. This view shows the original State House of 1792 with the dome and porch added by John Notman in 1847. The senate and assembly chambers occupied the main floor, and the governor's office and state library were on the second floor. This lithograph by J.R. Chapin appeared in an article on Trenton's buildings in Ballou's Pictorial Drawing Room Companion in 1855. (NJSM)

Right: The Emlen House on West State Street was built in 1796 and is an example of the stone townhouses that were built after Trenton had become the state capital. The Emlen family occupied the house for 90 years. During the 1920s it was known as "The Old Stone Tea House." Courtesy, Trentoniana Collection, TFPL

general store and residence at State and Warren streets. The information about Crolius is from a treasure-trove-like document dated October 13, 1783, which lists 28 householders (including two women, Charity Britton and Mary Barnes) in the town of Trenton and describes their dwelling places or accommodations. The list was compiled at a town meeting in the French Arms tavern, which was called to induce the Continental Congress to adjourn from Princeton (where they were already discussing departure) to Trenton. As a result, there exists a

document among the Papers of the Continental Congress that verbally sketches five Trenton residences owned by Stacy Potts, Jacob G. Bergen, George Ely, Alexander Chambers, and David Fick. George Ely's house was typical of the average residence: 32 by 18 feet, consisting of three stories of six rooms total, each with a fireplace, plus a kitchen, and filled with enough furniture for a small family. But it is the exact data on the Bergen property that sets the stage for the exciting period of the 1780s when the national government of the United States resided in Trenton. Indeed, the city was a contender for the permanent seat of the American government. And near the head of the list as possible government headquarters is a description of Bergen's place, from the October town meeting: "45 by 43 feet, 3 storeys, 11 rooms, 8 with fireplaces—a kitchen—and stabling for 12 horses," and his tavern's long room, which he offered for the meeting of the national Congress.

The city chosen as the center for the fledgling national government had to meet six specifications as described in a Maryland newspaper in July 1783:

1) It is neither a state capital nor commercial city
2) It must have access to navigable waters
3) It must receive prompt intelligence from all the states and from Europe
4) It must be in a state whose constitution guards against public turbulence
5) It must be centrally located geographically
6) It must be independent of all state and local jurisdiction

Several of these requirements were the direct result of the unhappy experiences Congressmen encountered in their Philadelphia meetings in late June when the beggared soldiers of the Pennsylvania Line surrounded Independence Hall. Happily for Trenton, the conditions aptly fit the area around the falls of the Delaware River.

It seems natural that Congress agreed to build the new national capital on the banks of the Delaware near Trenton in early October 1783 while meeting in nearby Princeton. The Southern delegation was so angered by this decision (one Virginia congressman wrote that any place in New Jersey was "execrable") that the Jersey delegation must have used their own state's experience to achieve a compromise. There was to be a dual capital system, as in colonial New Jersey, with the second capital to be on the Potomac River near Georgetown; Congress would alternate between the two capitals at least once every 12 months. The Geographer to the United States, Captain Thomas Hutchins, arrived in Trenton in early November with the Committee from the Congress, to survey the area from the Crosswicks to the Assunpink Creek, and submitted his map of the Lamberton area. His rough sketch of a triangular portion of Nottingham Township fronting on the Delaware is now in the Library of Congress. It shows an undeveloped area of 8,000 acres labeled as high, dry land, and so endowed with natural advantages that many national leaders viewed Trenton as their choice for a "capital place."

The Continental Congress did not actually meet in Trenton until a year later on November 1, 1784, when they convened in the long room of Bergen's French Arms tavern, specially leased for their use. Stacy Potts' house was occupied by the President of the Congress, Colonel Richard Lee, from November 30 to January 5, 1785, and other members resided in the accommodations offered previously. They were generally pleased with the area, voted $100,000 for buildings, and empowered three commissioners to enter into contracts for their construction before adjourning to New York

Patience Wright, 1725-1786, and her sister Rachel Wells were noted wax sculptors in the Trenton and Bordentown area. Patience gained fame, and her work was admired in New York, London, and Paris. This 1785 wax portrait of George Washington has been attributed to her and was once owned by Elias Boudinot, a president of the Continental Congress who resided in Bordentown. Courtesy, The Old Barracks Museum

City until the new buildings were ready. Almost immediately, George Washington (ever a Virginian) brought his personal influence to bear for a "more convenient . . . seat of the empire" by writing on February 8, 1785, to the president of the Congress criticizing the Lamberton choice. By September his endeavors were successful, as the capital ordinance was virtually repealed.

New Jersey—and Trenton—continued to propose the area on the Delaware as the logical choice for the national capital until 1801. In the last decade of the 18th century, the yellow fever epidemics in Philadelphia sent the federal government offices to the healthier environs of Trenton in 1793, 1797, and 1799. President John Adams, reluctant to leave his Massachusetts home, was finally convinced that he would not be "badly accommodated" in Trenton, and took an apartment in the Phoenix Hotel (Warren at West Hanover streets) in mid-October 1799, and conducted government business there for a brief period.

National leaders came to the Trenton vicinity for three reasons: because it was the seat of government, because they were traveling, and for social visits. Sometimes the visits were vacation trips by such luminaries as George Washington, who left Philadelphia in August 1787 for a long weekend fishing trip to Trenton. He lodged with Colonel Samuel Ogden near the ferry (where he wrote in his diary that the fishing was not very successful). After a Saturday which was spent above the town successfully catching perch, Washington dined with General Dickinson at his home, the Hermitage. He would write more extensively about his later, more formal visit in April 1789, when he was received by the white-robed choir of the matrons and young ladies of the area in front of the triumphal arch at the Assunpink Creek.

The names of those women who participated in this gala occasion have been preserved for posterity in our history books. Less well known is the name of Rachel Wells, a Trenton business owner and sculptor. She and her younger sister, Patience, grew up in Bordentown in the Quaker Lovell family and had similar talents as sculptors in wax. Patience would sail for England before the Revolutionary War and achieve renown as a wax modeler of such celebrities as King George III, Queen Charlotte, and Prime Minister William Pitt, the Earl of Chatham. Rachel's story is hinted at in her petitions to the state legislature in 1785 and 1787, when she eloquently pleaded with them to at least pay her interest on her considerable Revolutionary War loan to the state. The widow wrote in her unschooled scrawl that she had been stripped by the enemy during the war and could endure that distress more than she could bear the lack of common justice to her plea for financial repayment. In fragile health, Rachel had to abandon her waxworks, operated since pre-Revolutionary War days, with which she had supported herself and various nieces and nephews. Ever a shrewd businesswoman, Rachel's 1796 will removed her wax figures from her niece Sarah Wright to her brother John's custody since Sarah had shown herself to be too reckless to conduct the business on a money-making basis.

The women of the area enjoyed at least one special advantage as a result of the war—the 1776 New Jersey Constitution granted them suffrage provided they were Protestants and had at least £50. The large numbers of Quakers in the Trenton area, with their liberal views on women's equality, gave greater public assurance to the few women, usually widows or spinsters, who met the financial and religious qualifications, and chose to vote. Nonetheless, archival documents and newspapers of that day supply vivid descriptions of contested elections when individual women and blacks were challenged in their exercise of the ballot. Politics eventually intervened early in the 19th century and the suffrage clause was amended to include all white males, specifically excluding women and blacks.

The history of the number and life-styles of the region's black population has yet to be fully studied. There were several hundred non-whites in the immediate vicinity of Trenton, a number of whom were free. One, a local man named "Negro Prime," won his freedom in an unusual manner. Negro Prime had once been the illiterate slave of Loyalist Absalom Bainbridge of Lawrenceville, whose property was forfeited to the state when he "defected" to the British by moving to Long Island.

The New Jersey Supreme Court determined that Negro Prime was a slave of the state and was to be sold as their property, despite his service as a wagoneer for the American army. With an eloquent scribner petitioning the legislature on his behalf, Negro Prime appealed on the basis of liberty (the petition stated that "the fields of America have been dyed in the blood of her Citizens") and on the grounds of reasonable profit. Should he be sold, he argued, his price would scarcely amount to a fifth part of a copper penny to each taxpayer in the state, and Negro Prime could not believe that there was one person in New Jersey who would not willingly have contributed this small sum to release another human being from a life of bondage. It was not only the power of his words but also the support of prominent local men like Jacob Bergen and Moore Furman that released the state's slave by an act of the legislature on November 21, 1786—enabling Negro Prime to continue working in the Trenton area, now as a free man.

Within two decades, public sentiment throughout the state was strong enough to result in the passing of an act calling for the gradual abolition of slavery in New Jersey, although there were still at least 18 slaves in the state at the time of the Civil War (1860 census). Slave ownership had been a widespread practice among the wealthier families throughout New Jersey. In the Trenton area there are several references in wills and inventories, and in newspaper notices, to the practice of buying and sell-

ing blacks. Not all who lived in the Trenton area did so by choice.

As the 19th century came to the falls of the Delaware, the area presented the appealing view of a very quiet country town. Poplar trees lined the streets and the town's 3,000 inhabitants were scattered principally along Warren and State streets. Warren was the main thoroughfare and place of business. Observations of Trenton during this time were recorded in Stacy Gardner Potts' *Autobiography*. His initial impression of Trenton was often repeated by future generations who would see Trenton as a good place to live. In the summer of 1808 young Stacy Potts (then eight and a half years old) and his father walked from Harrisburg, Pennsylvania:

When, coming down the river from Yardleyville, we sat down to rest upon the bank opposite Trenton, and after my father had pointed out the different localities, I said "Well, I like the looks of that place, and think I shall live there all my life"—a thought probably become a fixed fact, for now though 52 years have passed, I live within a stone's throw of my first home here.

Throughout the postwar period, the city gradually added public improvements to enhance the commu-nity's growth. One such improvement was the remarka-ble wooden span over the Delaware River just below the falls, completed in 1806. Also, the community had es-tablished three local schools—the Trenton Academy for boys on Academy Street, the girls' academy in the brick schoolhouse on the Presbyterian Church ground, and the Friends' School taught in the second story of their meetinghouse at Hanover and Montgomery streets—although another school was needed for the children of the Lamberton and Mill Hill districts who could not afford the tuition these schools required. To meet this need, 65 inhabitants of the Township of Nottingham petitioned the state legislature to conduct a lottery to raise £250. Although they succeeded in raising the funds, it was another three decades before Trenton Township had a public school for poor children. There is evidence, though, that the town leaders had been con-cerned with the education of youth, even in the war years. In late November 1781, a Trenton paper carried a notice that a night school for English study would be opened in December at the brick schoolhouse near the Presbyterian Church. Apprentices and young workers would be attracted to this more practical education, and it served their needs better than the classical schooling that was the standard preparation for young gentlemen entering college and the professions.

Facing page: The first bridge across the Delaware at Trenton was a 1,100-foot covered wooden span, which was finished in 1806 at a cost of $180,000. The floor was suspended by iron rods hanging from the arches. The bridge was crossed by the tracks of the Philadelphia and Trenton railroad and withstood the flood of 1841 that swept other bridges away. Courtesy, Early Woodcut Views of New York and New Jersey, *Dover*

Below: In an issue of the New Jersey Gazette *in November 1786, Michael Forrest promised to instruct young gentlemen, for two dollars per quarter, in altimetry, longimetry, dialing, surveying, and navigation. The practical application of these subjects for employment is obvious. (NJSL)*

Bottom: The title of this 19th-century lithograph is "A view of Park Row at Trenton, New Jersey Embracing Six New Cottages erected by N. Hotchkiss and C. Thompson." They were near the New York and Philadelphia Railroad depot and the Delaware and Raritan Canal. The lithograph was drawn by A. Hoffy and published by Peter Duval in 1840. (NJHS)

NIHGT-SCHOOL.

THE fubfcriber began night-fchool at Trenton Academy, the 13th inftant, where he inftructs fuch young gentlemen as will attend, from fix till nine o'clock at night, in the following arts and fciences—reading, writing, arithmetic, geometry, trigonometry, altimetry, longimetry, dialing, menfuration, furveying, navigation, geography, &c. The price of tuition is two dollars per quarter; and the beft attention given to promote their learning, by their humble fervant,

MICHAEL FORREST.

Trenton, Nov. 11, 1786.   2w*

In the decade after the Revolutionary War, Isaac Collins' printing business in Trenton achieved a special renown with its beautifully typeset books. His 984-page publication of a quarto edition of the Holy Bible—the first one done in New Jersey and one of the earliest in America—was widely praised for its accuracy. Some have attributed this to a story that Collins paid his children for each error they detected, with the result that he had very motivated proofreaders and a fine reputation for his work.

Stacy Gardner Potts, who as a boy was delighted with the pleasant prospect of the town, brought special prominence to Trenton in June 1821 when he issued the first copy of the weekly literary paper, the *Emporium*, which had over 3,000 subscribers nationwide within two years. He continued to publish the paper until 1849.

Trenton became the site of the first state prison in 1799, but the prison soon proved to be a disgrace, and the legislature hired noted architect John Haviland to design a new prison. Built in South Trenton, the prison conformed to 18th-century reformer Jeremy Bentham's advanced penal reform concepts of light, ventilation, and exercise for the prisoners. The new structure opened in 1836. The joint legislative committee on the state prison in 1842 found that the prisoners were properly fed and clothed and were in good health.

In 1804 the Trenton Banking Company was organized and, after three years of effort, the Trenton Water Works was incorporated. An official Governor's Mansion was provided by the state, which purchased Moore Furman's house on State Street near Chancery Lane in 1798, since the legislature thought it proper that the state's chief executive and the heads of departments

should reside at the seat of government. That was not sufficient, however, to convince early 19th-century New Jersey governors, other than Richard Howell (1792-1801), to reside in Trenton. The mansion was finally sold in 1845, after which governors rented hotel rooms or commuted from their homes to their offices in the State House.

By 1792 the area at the falls of the Delaware had at least achieved a compact civic identity as the City of Trenton, something the residents had sought in various proposals to the state legislature since 1786. One unsuccessful proposal, supported by 219 signatures, was to incorporate the townships of Hopewell, Maidenhead, and Trenton into a single borough, with the inducement of assuming the support of the courthouse and jail in Trenton. With the designation of Flemington as the Hunterdon County Seat in 1791, the building sat vacant in the midst of a thriving business district. It was sold in

1805 to the newly formed Trenton Banking Company, having seen service as a site for Baptist services and city government meetings. With their own municipal government, Trentonians soon acquired a plow and other implements for repairing their streets.

Evidence that the Royal Borough of Trenton still existed in the minds of the residents is the 1786 petition to unite the Burlington County Township of Nottingham with the Hunterdon County Township of Trenton to create a City of Trenton. The petition was rejected by the state assembly but the colonial hamlets of Mill Hill, Bloomsbury, and Trenton Ferry in Nottingham Township were united to form the Borough of South Trenton.

The county line along Assunpink Creek presented an unnatural division between Hunterdon and Burlington as the population stretched out along the roadway patterns from the old village cores. Local discontent with

Facing page: The first Roman Catholic church in New Jersey, built in 1814, was St. John's. In 1848 a new St. John's Church (shown here) was erected at Broad and Centre streets. Built in the prevailing Greek Revival style of the city's Protestant churches, this church was lost in a fire and was replaced in 1889 by the Sacred Heart Church. Courtesy, Trentoniana Collection, TFPL

Right: The banks in Trenton in the 19th century printed their own money as was the practice in many cities. The one-dollar bill shows a small engraving of the 1806 bridge across the Delaware, and the two-dollar bill of the City Bank

of Trenton depicts an early railroad locomotive at the station. (NJHS)

Below: This woodcut from Barber and Howe's history shows the Trenton State Prison soon after it was built in 1836. The Delaware and Raritan Canal and the Camden and Amboy Railroad ran along the line of the front wall. Visible behind the wall are the main building where the keeper and the staff lived and the roofs of the corridors that contained the prisoners' cells. Courtesy, Early Woodcuts of New York and New Jersey, Dover

the 50-year-old boundaries of the 13 colonial counties finally found a sympathetic ear in the state legislature. With a typical political solution, new counties were then incorporated along partisan lines since each served as the sole election district for a member of the oligarchical state senate. The 13 senators increased by two, and then the central New Jersey county of Mercer—named for the Revolutionary War general who had fallen at the Battle of Princeton—was created in 1838 to balance the more northern Hudson County, making an even number of counties: 16.

Political expediency made it necessary to pass two leg-islative acts to carve the new county from parts of Hunterdon, Burlington, Middlesex, and Somerset. The Somerset County legislators would only vote for Mercer's creation if no part of their territory was given to it. Once the Hunterdon/Burlington/Middlesex piece was voted on, the Somerset legislators were out-maneuvered when a second bill took a portion of their county to round out Mercer's northeastern border.

Trenton was once again a county seat. But now it was the seat of a new, 19th-century county which was embarking on the adventure of becoming a magnet for the state's industry and commerce.

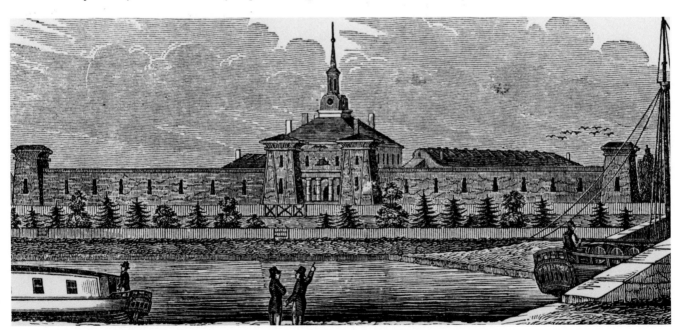

Chapter Four

CANAL TOWN TO INDUSTRIAL CENTER

The close bond between transportation and commerce can be seen in this late-19th-century photograph of the John A. Roebling and Sons works. The Camden and Amboy Railroad and the Delaware and Raritan Canal lie just outside the factory wall. Courtesy, Trentoniana Collection, TFPL

In the 19th century, Trenton's story was based on the successes achieved by enterprising men who took advantage of the national economic climate to transform Trent's village into an industrial city.

Newly perfected technologies made it possible to overcome the impediment of limited water supply that had thwarted the growth of industries in Trenton prior to 1830 when water was the chief source of industrial power. In 1830, the area known today as Trenton had a population estimated at 4,561 people. There were about 712 residences with an average occupancy of six to seven persons, for Trenton city proper, Mill Hill, Bloomsbury, and Lamberton. Census records and Thomas F. Gordon's *Gazetteer of the State of New Jersey* also contain evidence about the industrial component of this region: for example, there were five flour mills, two on the Assunpink Creek between South Broad and South Warren streets, another at the foot of Mill Street on the Delaware, and two in the Millham settlement further up on the Assunpink. There were two sawmills on Petty's Run and another near the flour mills at Millham. A paper mill was built about 1812 on Petty's Run, too, which continued to make paper and related products until 1877.

The leading new industry in the early decades of the 19th century was cotton processing, and the Trenton area could boast at least four cotton mills with a total of 200 looms near the Assunpink between South Broad and Warren streets. All of the land west of Calhoun Street, north of the Battle Monument, and east of Stockton Street was rural—a panorama of farms, woodlands, a few scattered crossroad villages and an occasional mill. The soil was sufficiently fertile and the farmers knowledgeable enough to produce a large surplus quantity of grain, which was readily marketed in New York City or Philadelphia.

By the second decade of the 19th century, it had become obvious that the water power in the vicinity of Trenton, while being used to full capacity, would not fulfill the city's growing needs. A private group, the Trenton Delaware Falls Company, began construction of a remedy in 1831, the Trenton Water Power canal (known locally as the Water Power). With a minimum depth of six feet, the Trenton Water Power raceway began at a wing dam upriver at Scudder's Falls, ran south close to the Delaware for almost seven miles, then via an aqueduct over the Assunpink Creek into south Trenton where it emptied into the Delaware at several points.

The 1834 New Jersey gazetteer of Thomas F. Gordon reflects the national trend toward canal building, which many cities saw as the solution to their transportation problems. Boldly, Gordon publicly writes of the not "very thriving state" of Trenton but how the new enterprise—the Water Power—had improved the business tempo of the town. Thirty-seven years later, in 1871, another local writer, John O. Raum, concluded about the Water Power: "It has been the means of building up a large and prosperous business in our city, much of which we could not have had but for the facilities afforded by it. On its banks are erected many mills, some of which are very extensive."

Although started in 1830, the Delaware and Raritan Canal was not finished until 1838, four years after the Trenton Water Power was completed. The value of Trenton's position between the major cities of New York and Philadelphia was demonstrated once again when the more desirable all-water connection became a reality in the early 19th century. Not only would the Delaware and Raritan Canal pass through Trenton, but its 22-mile long feeder canal (which maintained the water level) would also bisect the area, providing an efficient transportation link to the major city markets within 60 miles.

A large basin for canal boats was constructed on the feeder near West Hanover and Montgomery streets. Where the feeder joined the main canal near Perry and North Clinton avenues, there was another basin, which soon became known as Coalport. Trenton's strategic position at the intersection of the canal and feeder made it economically attractive for receiving raw material and fuels—those bulky, heavy cargoes most suitable for water-borne transport. At Trenton the barges of coal from the Lehigh area of northern Pennsylvania encouraged the establishment of factories, many of which had their own basins and docks. The canal itself was a source of several hundred jobs for the men and boys of Trenton, who worked as mule drivers or stablers, lock operators, boat captains, and maintenance workers.

It was inevitable that railroads would enter the city, especially since the trains run in nearby Bordentown and in Hoboken were among the earliest in America. By 1837, local men had organized the Philadelphia and Trenton Railroad to lay tracks from the Morrisville depot to Trenton, across the Delaware Bridge. The line extended from the river to the west bank of the Delaware and Raritan Canal, and through the city to the

UNION LINE
TRENTON

COACHES.

THE Citizens of Trenton, its vicinity, and the Public generally, are respectfully informed, that the STEAMBOAT has commenced running.

—Leaving Trenton, Every Day, at 1 o'clock, P. M. and on returning will leave Philadelphia at 6 o'clock, A. M. Sundays excepted.

Good Coaches with careful drivers, will be ready to convey Passengers to the Steamboat. All passengers for the above Line, will please to have their names on the Book at the Union Line Office, and will be called for at their residences, (at any reasonable distance.)

☞ All baggage at the owners risk.

A. P. ATKINSON, Agent.
Trenton, Feb. 13, 1832.   33-tf.

Trenton Prices Current.

WHEAT	106	RYE	75 to 80
CORN	53	OATS	43
BUTTER	16	EGGS	20
FLAXSEED	1 70	MUSTARDSEED	4 50

Apprentices Indentures,
For Sale at this office.

Delaware and Raritan Canal.

NOTICE IS HEREBY GIVEN, That the Canal will be open for vessels drawing 6 feet water, on the 16th day of March next, if the weather does not prevent.

The depth of water in the Canal will be gradually increased, of which due notice will be given.

JOHN R. THOMPSON, Sec'ry.
February 16, 1835.   297-tf.

Trenton station at East Hanover and North Broad streets. The next year, 1838, the Camden and Amboy Railroad connected Bordentown through Trenton to Kingston and also New Brunswick, with a depot in Trenton on East State Street. In the decades of the 1840s and 1850s, other companies built lines north along the Delaware River to tap the coal fields of the Manuka Chunk area, while the lines to Philadelphia and New York gave railway access to the population centers of the nation. In the mid-19th century, railroad service was primarily for passengers, with what freight there was handled on the regular passenger cars. The canal was the mode most suited to freight transport, its passenger service declining with the spreading network of railroads until only picnickers and special excursionists travelled by canal boat.

In the spring of 1842 when the author-illustrator team of John W. Barber and Henry Howe toured Mercer County, they observed that the localities of Mill Hill, Bloomsbury, and Lamberton—combined in the borough of South Trenton and extending almost a mile south of the Assunpink Creek—should be considered part of the city of Trenton. In their book, *Historical Collections of the State of New Jersey,* they write that this area's combined population was upwards of 6,000 out of the county's total of 21,075. Lamberton had about 70 dwellings, Mill Hill about 80, and Bloomsbury almost 150 residences.

Surrounding municipalities offer comparative statistics. Ewing, formed from Trenton Township in 1834, had a population of 1,017, with one fulling mill, one woolen factory, one grist- and two sawmills, and a capital investment in manufacturing of $14,500; Ewing's three schools served 77 students. Rural Hopewell supported 3,213 residents and consisted of five separate villages, none of which contained any manufacturing plants but did offer their residents stores, taverns, and a number of "mechanic shops." Lawrence Township, with a population of 1,556, had a manufacturing capital investment of $14,600 in one sawmill and three gristmills; its two schools served 92 children. Nottingham Township, which in 1840 included Hamilton and the borough of South Trenton, was primarily an industrial area with three iron furnaces, three fulling mills, three woolen mills, seven sawmills, seven cotton factories, five tanneries, ten gristmills, and one oil mill as evidence of its sizeable capital investment of $596,700. Nottingham Township's residents were served by 28 stores, and the records show that in 1840 its 13 schools enrolled 348 students, with 36 in a private academy. Considering the figures given for the neighboring townships, it is easy to understand why Nottingham Township divided into thirds in 1842.

Trenton proper was the obvious commercial center of the county in 1842, with its 50 retail stores (worth $196,300), two banks, numerous public buildings, four academies (104 students), ten schools (314 students), a lyceum, and eleven churches. The manufacturing sector of the city was a distant second to Nottingham with three tanneries, a brewery, a pottery, three paper factories, a rope walk, two flouring mills, two gristmills, three

Facing page top: Even before the advent of canals and railroads, Trentonians were served by the coaches and steamboats of the Union Line. This notice, from the New Jersey State Gazette *of February 13, 1832, shows the state of the rural economy of the region through its list of current prices. (NJSL)*

Facing page bottom: After the Delaware and Raritan Canal opened in 1838, the New Jersey State Gazette *frequently printed advertisements for the waterway. The depth of the canal determined the size of boats that could be used, as larger vessels drew more water. (NJSL)*

Right: The water links of river, creek, and canal are clearly seen in this map of Trenton in 1835. The Trenton and New Brunswick and the Princeton and Kingston turnpikes also brought the outlying regions into Trenton's commercial orbit. (NJSL)

Below: This 1900 photograph shows the steamer Raritan *leaving lock 7 at State Street. Built by Pusey and Jones in Wilmington, Delaware, in 1858, the 167-ton steamer, which was operated from Trenton, was finally abandoned in 1917. Courtesy, Trentoniana Collection, TFPL*

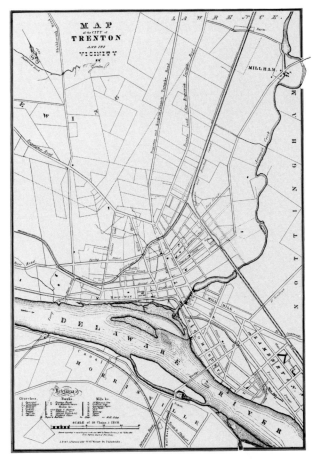

Above: When Peter Grim, Jr., built the Tremont House in 1847, the Camden and Amboy railroad station and lock 7 of the Delaware and Raritan Canal were nearby. In 1848 Henry Clay gave a speech from the second-story balcony to a cheering crowd of spectators. The view is from a business card issued by Joseph Cunningham in the 1850s. The building still stands at the corner of East State and West Canal streets. Courtesy, Trentoniana Collection, TFPL

Facing page top: The Trenton Brewing Company on Lalor Street in South Trenton once drew water from the Delaware for its malt liquors. Steamers carried materials to the dock below the bluff at the river's edge. Courtesy, Trentoniana Collection, TFPL

Facing page bottom: The establishment of the South Trenton Iron Company by Peter Cooper in 1845 boosted the development of Trenton as one of the nation's leading industrial centers. The names of Cooper, Hewitt, and Roebling were soon associated with the rising prosperity of the city. Courtesy, Trentoniana Collection, TFPL

sawmills, three printing offices, two binderies, and three newspapers worth a total capital of $277,800.

The decade of the 1840s was an important period for attracting new major industries to Trenton, probably best exemplified by the success of Peter Cooper. The New York businessman established the South Trenton Iron Company (a rolling mill) in 1845 at the foot of Warren Street. The location was the American Bridge site along the Delaware, recognizable today by the landmark two-story red brick building. Incorporated in 1847, the Trenton Iron Works spawned the nearby New Jersey Steel and Iron Company after the Civil War. These immense mills were in the forefront of the technological advancement of metallurgy. The first of Amer-

ica's iron structural beams and seven-inch rail beams were rolled at the Trenton Mill in the 1850s. Here also occurred some of the first experiments in the refining of iron into steel by the Bessemer process. Cooper, who had investments in New York, Baltimore, and Phillipsburg, as well as in Ringwood, New Jersey, and Durham, Pennsylvania, found the Trenton location so conducive to his business that he convinced John A. Roebling to move his wire rope business to Trenton in 1848. With the engineering success of the Brooklyn Bridge, dedicated in 1883, Trenton provided jobs for Italian and Slavic immigrants in the wire rope works of John A. Roebling Sons. Their factory occupied a large tract between South Broad Street and Clinton Avenue. Eventually the Roeblings were responsible for building an entire town a few miles south on the Delaware River, which they named, appropriately, "Roebling." Adding to the city's commercial ventures, the Phoenix Iron Works expanded from an axe factory to a machine shop and iron foundry in 1849.

The United States Census provides a basis for describing the generally flourishing atmosphere of Trenton at mid-century. The population growth between 1840 and 1850 was an astounding 58 percent increase to 6,461, with a separate count for "colored" at 526 (representing a 19 percent growth in population). Local daily newspapers reported considerable building in the Trenton area

and wrote that more than 60 new houses had been completed in one year. From governmental buildings and mills, the small town on the banks of the Delaware was rapidly developing into an iron and steel factory center with a pool of workers anxious for jobs.

Most of the iron-working establishments were located in the area south of the Assunpink Creek, a clustering that shows their interdependence. But their successful operation is also attributable to the geographical factors of the area; here was a location which contained sources of power, water, and transportation facilities for raw materials and for massive finished products, on low-lying, level ground which was open, and reasonably priced.

Iron manufacturing, Trenton's first major industry, continued to be a significant industry in the area for the next 100 years, and a major power in the economy and work force that developed. It grew with the city as the nation grew: in 1860 there were 23 iron businesses and by 1890 there were 40 iron establishments employing 1,361 workers. By 1910 just one of those firms, the Fisher and Norris Anvil Works, employed over 300 men and boys. Founder Mark Fisher established the company in Trenton in 1843 to introduce the first American-made anvils. The Fisher and Norris factory also made the first metal clamps to hold railroad tracks together; they were known as "fish plates," a name supposedly derived from the firm's name. In addition to its unique products, the firm achieved a special recognition because of its owner-manager, Mrs. Harriet Fisher, who later supervised the foundry's operations from 1902 to 1939. Nicknamed the "Anvil Queen" and "The Iron Woman," Fisher was also a world traveller, author, and ardent automobile promoter.

By the time of the Civil War, the iron industries had supplanted the earlier predominance of the cotton and woolen mills. The new "heavy" manufacturing companies provided employment for the male population while female workers and children found work in the textile industry. The mills usually worked with both cotton and woolen textiles, and were more dispersed than the iron works. In 1860 Samuel K. Wilson's Woolen Mill was the largest, employing 160 people in its building on the south side of the creek. Another woolen mill was located nearby on Cooper Street not far from one of Trenton's three carpet-weaving shops. The city had two shirt factories and a complex of textile mills near the southern terminus of the Water Power that included,

prior to 1850, a calico print works and the Saxony Mills, which produced stockings and shirts. Whitehead and Sons established a woolen shirt factory outside the town (on the Assunpink Creek just beyond the small settlement at Millham) in 1842. After 1869, the Whitehead Company pioneered in the rubber industry by which it gained its long life. During the decade 1850-1860, the rubber industry had begun in Trenton on a small scale with two factories. In 1854 one firm located on Third Street in south Trenton, while another was established in 1856 on North Clinton Avenue: they produced rubber dolls, belting, and blankets. During the Civil War years, the Star Rubber Works was established in the city. The rubber works were usually located in the same industrial areas of Trenton as the potteries and so provided a choice of work for the mainly English residents there. The location of three rubber works east of the city limits by 1890 reflects their outward migration, a trend that continued into the early 20th century. In Hamilton Township were the Whitehead and the Trenton (Thermoid) Companies, with the community of Hamilton Square claiming another rubber works. Ewing Township had two such factories, both started in the 1880s and both on Prospect Street.

Prior to the Civil War, women had also found work in Trenton's only food canning plant, which was started about 1836 on South Stockton Street between State and Front streets. In 1860 the plant employed 35 women and 6 men.

The growth of local industry from 1860 to 1890 is shown in Jesse Turk's study of Trenton. (Table 1).

Table 1
Industrial Establishments

	1860	1890
Iron Working	23	40
Textile	7	59
Clay and Pottery	10	15
Woodworking	21	30
Food Processing	8	23
Leather working	49	7
Paper	4	5
Rubber	2	13
Other	25	69
TOTAL	149	261
Newspaper (daily, Sunday, weekly)	4	14

Source: Jesse Rose Turk, "Trenton, New Jersey in the Nineteenth Century."

In response to the new industrial establishments, and to the large immigration from Ireland and Germany, there was a major population increase for the Trenton area in the mid-19th century. By 1860 the federal census credits the city with 17,228 people, a 166.6 percent increase. This was due, in part, to the city's annexation of the populous boroughs of South Trenton (1851) and Lamberton (1856).

An inspection of the original census survey lists reveals that, not surprisingly, many residents were now born in Ireland or one of the German states. The newcomers found homes in recently built two-to-three story houses within walking distance of the factories, which were for the most part located south of Assunpink Creek and east to about Clinton Avenue. Upper-class housing was being built between Willow and Calhoun streets, creating an impressive setting for the expanding State House. By 1860 a new neighborhood of large single-family homes was being developed on North Clinton Avenue around the State Normal School established

Above: Rubber manufacturing plants were among Trenton's primary industries in the late 1800s. The Empire Rubber Company occupied 27 acres of land and had outlet stores in Chicago and New York. The company produced fire, mill, and garden hoses, belting, gaskets, valves, ducks, mats, and bicycle tires. Courtesy, Trentoniana Collection, TFPL

Below: In keeping with the national trend toward educational reform, the first state normal school was founded at Trenton in 1855. This view of the campus was taken in 1890. After becoming Trenton State College, the campus was moved to the present location in Ewing Township. Courtesy, Trentoniana Collection, TFPL

Facing page: Trentonians were supplied with fresh bread each day by the proud fleet of horse-drawn wagons of Hill's Bakery. Trenton became renowned as a center of bakeries, breweries, and sausage manufacturing. Courtesy, Trentoniana Collection, TFPL

there in 1855. The area from East State to approximately Perry Street, and from Carroll eastward to Clinton, became a desirable location for the houses of the upper middle class of mill owners. Several, such as the Masonic Scottish Rite building and the Mount Carmel Guild, still survive, and are noted for their ornate Victorian interiors.

When President-elect Abraham Lincoln visited Trenton on February 21, 1861, on the way to his inauguration, he saw a Trenton that had maintained its significance as a governmental, trade, and traveller-service community. However, it was also acquiring the dispersed factories and varied levels of housing characteristic of an emerging industrial city. But, according to local historian John Raum, Trentonians, recollecting their town at that time, would look back in 1882 and describe it as "a sleepy, old-fashioned town, that had reposed . . . in rather proud old fogyism for two hundred years."

The U.S. Census figures, which show a 300 percent increase in the population from 1840 to 1860, disprove the view that pre-Civil War Trenton was stagnant. During these decades, however, the city did visibly change its appearance in comparison to the bucolic small town viewed by Stacy Gardner Potts in the early years of the century. By the 1880s there was dense land occupancy in the older city core made possible by the introduction of brick row housing. Population growth, especially from recent European immigration, increased the need for the development of open spaces for housing. The Borough of Chambersburg and the Township of Millham were

annexed to the city of Trenton in 1888. The steady increase of industrial firms expanded the commercial area of Trenton, and the contiguous regions of Ewing, Hamilton, and Lawrence townships merged into the industrial and residential scene so that political boundaries were not readily apparent in the streetscapes.

The 19th century was marked by years of depressions and recession unrelieved by federal social welfare programs, and Trenton experienced its share of economic hard times. Counterfeiting was widespread since there was no national currency system and banks circulated their own notes. Tellers at Trenton's banks were esteemed for their ability to detect counterfeit notes and the banks' records include frequent mention of the crime.

Today's Trenton Soup Kitchen had its early counterpart in the 1855 Trenton Soup House which distributed 240 quarts of soup daily. The local papers tell of the general suffering of the community that year and of the incessant requests for relief at the mayor's office. Private charitable agencies like the Female Benevolent Society and the Dorcas Society solicited commercial firms such as the Trenton Banking Company to continue their sporadic assistance to the most needy cases. A history of the Trenton Banking Company points with pride to newspaper references to the prudent management of local banks, which had stood firm in the panic of 1837 and were still strong despite the country-wide suspension of specie payment, the exchange of paper money for gold or silver.

Facing page: The Trenton Lamp Company, located on Ingham Avenue, produced ceramic globe lamps. Male and female employees adorned the globes with delicate, hand-painted floral patterns. Courtesy, Trentoniana Collection, TFPL

Above: This 1899 photograph shows a steam locomotive on the Belvidere Division hauling a freight train along the edge of Cadwalader Park. The train is passing a white wooden swing bridge over the Delaware and Raritan Canal feeder. By the turn of the century railroads linked Trenton with many of its satellite communities. Courtesy, Trentoniana Collection, TFPL

The efforts of the laboring class to gain more humane working conditions and a higher standard of living saw the establishment of unions. The printing trade was unionized during the Civil War but the most active unions were in the potteries. The entire community suffered when the Knights of Labor went on strike in the decades between the Civil War and the turn of the century. The strikes gradually improved the potters' conditions, but the long-term effect was the strangulation of the potteries, many of which left the area. This pattern was—and is still—being repeated by industries that could easily find new locations where, as in Trenton during the wave of immigration, there existed a large pool of poor workers anxious to work.

As a result of industrialization, changes in the social fabric of the area became apparent in the extensive public school construction that occurred in the 1880s in response to the flood of immigrants who had to be "Americanized." Eight new elementary schools were built in the city itself. A second school for black children was completed in the Seventh Ward, north of Assunpink Creek. In the old residential area of Mill Hill, the first public high school was dedicated in the fall of 1874.

Various state institutions were erected on the city's outskirts—the School for the Deaf (1833), the State Hospital (1848), the first State Normal School (1855), and the State Home for Girls (1871). These were soon engulfed by the area's new housing, which replaced the interdependent agricultural belt that had separated the city from the crossroad settlements. Some of the identities of former outlying villages are retained in place names such as West Trenton, White Horse, and Mercerville, while others such as Millham Junction, Hillwood Lakes, Lawrence Mills, and Port Mercer exist only in the recollections of older residents.

Street railways were extended from the commercial and factory areas into the residential districts. By the 1870s land companies were buying up farms and large estates and developing them into blocks of new houses, mostly for working-class families. Thus people could live farther from their jobs, and more students could travel to the city's high school, which instituted a commercial course as an alternative to the traditional academic course work. The new residential area called for churches and civic services, such as the elementary schools and firehouses already provided in the downtown area, paving the way for the suburban growth experienced after the First and Second World Wars. The diffusion of the population and the new institutions broadened the area known as Trenton into the adjoining townships. The residents there continued to think of themselves as Trentonians.

Chapter Five

THE STAFFORDSHIRE OF AMERICA

by Ellen and Bert Denker

This wood engraving from Frank Leslie's Illustrated Newspaper, *June 23, 1888, shows the various trades employed in the potteries of Trenton. Watching over all of the activities from the upper right is Isaac Broome's famous bust of Cleopatra. (NJSM)*

*L*ong ago Trenton earned its title, the "Staffordshire of America." As the analogy suggests, Trenton had become the most active center of ceramic production in the United States by 1880, in much the same way that the Staffordshire district was and continues to be the ceramic center of England. The outlook for Trenton's burgeoning ceramic industry was so bright in the 1880s some commentators including a writer for an 1880 issue of *Harper's New Monthly Magazine,* felt "that, in the not distant future, Staffordshire may be spoken of as the Trenton of England." Every kind of ware made in America from the late 1700s to the present has been made in Trenton, including bricks, redware, stoneware, yellow ware, ironstone, table and art porcelain, sanitary ware, tile, architectural terra-cotta, and art pottery.

There are many reasons why the industry prospered on the banks of the Delaware River. Good transportation systems were established early. With canals, railroads, and roadways, raw materials from near and far were cheaply imported. Clays came from South Carolina and Florida; flint and spar from Maine, Connecticut, Maryland, and Delaware; fine china clays from England; and coal from Pennsylvania to fire the kilns. Finished products were conveniently exported across the country wherever the railroads reached. However, location and transportation alone cannot account for the enormous success of the ceramic industry in Trenton. Certainly there were other cities with these same advantages.

The most compelling reason for Trenton's rise to prominence in the ceramic industry is that accomplishment breeds prosperity. The good fortune of the English potters who came to Trenton during the 1850s because of its proximity to markets attracted more English potters anxious to leave the highly competitive industry in Staffordshire. Trenton's entrepreneurs saw the value of financing these new ventures and thereby perpetuated the prosperous atmosphere with ready capitalization. Within this complex interrelationship continuity was the prime ingredient. Industry thrives through experimentation built upon expertise, as well as the presence of support services and a large pool of skilled workers from which to draw. From 1870 onward, Trenton's potters have been on the horizon of the American ceramic industry. To name all of the literally hundreds of individual potteries that have operated is beyond the scope of this chapter. The history of the industry in Trenton is very complex because the stories of many potteries are intertwined. Owners, whether they were practical potters or financial backers, often formed several partnerships during their careers in the ceramic industry in Trenton. In the next few pages, however, the major personalities and changes in the industry will be explored.

There was little about Trenton's inauspicious beginnings in ceramic production to suggest what lay ahead. In the 18th and early 19th centuries potters fulfilled only local needs in the same way that pottery was made and marketed in hundreds of other areas in America. The largest clay deposits in the area were most suitable for brick and terra-cotta manufacture. Pleistocene-era clays along Princeton Avenue and Raritan clays along Pond Run east of the city were exploited by brickmakers and early potters.

A Mr. Emly is identified as Trenton's first brickmaker in about 1817. John Smith established a brickyard near the clay deposits along Princeton Avenue at about the same time. From 1824 to 1842 Morgan Beakes, who was also a farmer, manufactured about 300,000 bricks a year. As the city grew the brickmaking business increased during the second half of the 19th century until, by 1890, 13 brickyards were pressing more than 30 million bricks per year in the Trenton area. Others engaged in the business included Samuel Mulford, Peter Grim, George Kulp, Peter and Daniel Fell, Joseph Hymer, Henry Nice, William King, Joseph Boud, Charles Garrot, and F.D. Cook.

Coarse red earthenwares were cheaply made from common materials obtained close at hand and satisfied the needs of local residents for kitchen and dairy crockery. The making of redware was usually a second occupation for most potters who combined their potting skills with seasonal activities such as farming. James Rhodes, whose "Pot-Works" in the Bloomsbury section of Trenton was for sale in 1787; John Morton, who had an "Earthen-Ware Manufactory" on the Pennington road two miles from Trenton before 1828, and Jacob Haster & Sons, who offered "Earthenware of the best quality" in 1817 may have had additional occupations.

The McCullys, on the other hand, are a conspicuous exception for pottery was their sole business. Joseph McCully (1757-1820) and his nephew, Joseph McCully (1771-1857), made lead-glazed red earthenware with slip decoration from about 1784 until 1849. John Stiles McCully, son of the younger Joseph, continued the business from 1849 until he sold the land on Union Street in 1868 to Father Anthony Smith for St. Mary's School.

Unlike the making of redware, production of grey salt-glazed stoneware required specialization. Few potters could make stoneware as a part-time occupation because stoneware clays came only from distant locations and were costly to transport compared to the redware clays obtained locally. Bernard Hanlon's 1780 advertisement in the *New Jersey Gazette* offered "a good assortment of Stone Ware; Potts, Jugs, Mugs and Pans of different sizes" which he sold "on very modest terms, for cash or country produce." The pottery was part of Hanlon's Mills near where the Assunpink Creek and North Clinton Avenue (later called Millham) intersect. The grist mill and sawmill were in operation for many years while the pottery is mentioned only in advertisements from 1778 to 1780.

By the second quarter of the 19th century redwares were being replaced as common household crockery by yellow earthenwares and buff stonewares decorated with clear or brown-spotted glazes. The brown-spotted ware was called "Rockingham" because of its origins in that area of England.

White earthenwares were made to look like porcelain but were much heavier and lacked the translucency characteristic of porcelain. In terms of production, white ware differs from yellow ware only in the color of clays and glazes used. In the mid-19th-century home yellow wares were used for kitchen crockery such as bowls,

Above: The availability of good transportation systems aided the development of the pottery industry in Trenton, as this view of the pottery district along the railroad and canal illustrates. The periodic kilns burned coal, and that fuel was delivered by rail or water. "Above all," wrote Woodward and Hageman in their 1883 history of Trenton, "towers the ever present chimney, sending forth, like the crater of a volcano, its large volume of dark-colored smoke." (NJSM)

Facing page: Workers carry saggers into the kiln at the Lenox factory about 1923. Saggers are clay boxes that are filled with ware to be fired. Stacked neatly inside the kiln, the saggers prevented a single accident in the firing from destroying all or part of a load. Local boys nicknamed the English pottery workers in Trenton "cheeseheads" because the saggers look like great wheels of cheese. (NJSM)

pitchers, and pie plates, while white wares decorated the dining table.

Most yellow and white earthenwares were molded rather than wheel-thrown as the earlier redwares and stonewares generally were. The processes involved in making molded wares required a division of labor within the factory because large quantities of the ware had to be made in order for the business to be profitable. Clays were brought from different sources and more care was taken in their preparation at the pottery. Design and fabrication of molds was a specialized skill, as were the processes of molding wares (by casting or pressing), finishing the greenware by fettling and sponging, glazing the ware, placing it in kilns, and firing the kilns. These skills were learned in the Staffordshire potteries and

brought to America by men like William Young, James Taylor, John Astbury, and Richard Millington, all of whom had settled in Trenton by 1860.

Prior to 1880 most of the finer ceramics used in American homes came from England and, to a lesser extent, Germany, France, and China. American manufacturers and foreign-born makers who immigrated to the United States were anxious to produce ceramics for the expanding American population, but foreign wares flooded home markets at prices much lower than would be profitable for manufacture of the same goods here.

The atmosphere changed radically after 1860, however. Beginning in 1861 protectionist tariffs imposed on foreign ceramics provided an environment that was far more conducive to profitability in American potteries. Although the Civil War had slowed production in most industries, American business boomed after 1865. In Trenton, all of the elements that enabled the city to become the "Staffordshire of America" were in place by the end of the Civil War.

The earliest of the English potters to work in Trenton before 1860 was James Taylor (1810-1887), a native of Staffordshire. He came to America in 1829 and worked in potteries in Jersey City, New Jersey; Troy, Indiana; Osville, Kentucky; and Cincinnati, Ohio, before settling in East Liverpool, Ohio, to make yellow ware for eight years. In 1852 he began construction of a pottery on Taylor and Jackson streets in Trenton with his associate, Henry Speeler, a continental potter from East Liverpool. Taylor continued with several different partners in the manufacture of whiteware until he finally sold out to Isaac Davis in 1875.

Other earthenware manufacturers during this period include the Trenton City Pottery of James Yates and Frederick A.F. Titus; George Lawton and his sons James and George, Jr.; Richard Millington; Lawton and I.W. Cory; and the Assunpink Pottery Works of Henry Speeler and his sons.

By 1855, the common ware of choice was variously called ironstone, white granite, stone china, or opaque porcelain. Though white in color, this ware is basically a refined earthenware that lacks the translucency of porcelain. It is not entirely clear which pottery was the first to make white granite wares in Trenton. According to John Raum's *History of Trenton* (1871) credit should go to the pottery of James Yates and William Rhodes in about 1859, although claims of first are always open to ques-

tion. In 1856, Yates and Nelson Large, of Lambertville, purchased William Young & Co.'s pottery on Perry Street. Yates and his subsequent partner, Rhodes, enlarged the works in 1859 "and commenced the manufacture of white earthenware, white granite and cream-colored ware."

The East Trenton Porcelain Company was incorporated in 1864 with a capital stock of $100,000 to make white granite wares. A description of the company's physical layout in 1871 presents a picture of a pottery operation in Trenton during this period: The company had four kilns and four buildings two stories high, two kiln sheds, a mill room, clay sheds, and a frit-kiln room; slip kilns and a packing room comprised the work space. A half basin along the canal assured easy transportation of raw materials and finished goods. Raum describes the complex in his history of Trenton: "Twelve brick tenement-houses, three stories high, with three rooms on each floor, and cellars under the whole, are also connected with the works and are occupied by the workmen and their families; these, with a barn eighteen feet high, forty by fifty feet, built of brick and used as a stable for horses and for storage, with a frame wagon shed adjoining . . . make quite a respectable village. . . . They have the largest packing-house in Trenton, with cellar for hogsheads, and also a cellar under the northwest building for the storage of prepared clay."

Many manufacturers of yellow ware made white ware also. James Taylor and Henry Speeler and the Trenton City Pottery of Yates and Titus have been mentioned. Richard Millington, John Astbury, and several other partners advertised "White Stone China" as a product of the Carroll Street Pottery. Millington, Astbury, and Theophilus Poulson may be credited with making the

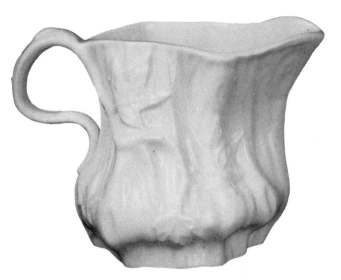

earliest datable white ware for their "Ellsworth Pitcher" of 1861. Other potteries that turned out white ware during the 1860s and 1870s include Brearley and Stephens; the Glasgow Pottery of John Moses; Coxon and Thompson; the Greenwood Pottery; and the Etruria Works.

Of all the ceramic bodies, porcelain is the most difficult and costly to produce. American earthenwares and stonewares are generally made of coarse clays, while porcelain is made from a variety of fine white clays. Whiteness and translucency make porcelain the most desirable of all ceramics.

William H. Young, Sr. (1801-1871), a potter from Staffordshire, was manager in the porcelain doorknob department of Charles Cartlidge & Company at Greenpoint, Long Island when Charles Hattersley persuaded him to move to Trenton in 1853. Hattersley, a cutler by trade from Connecticut, specialized in door locks. Young made porcelain doorknobs as well as escutcheons, doorplates, and harness furniture in his pottery on Perry Street. Despite the mundane nature of most of their work Young and his sons received the first premium from the Franklin Institute, Philadelphia, in 1854 "for the splendid specimens of Porcelain Ware manufactured at their establishment." A large porcelain pitcher with ivy in relief made about this time is considered to be Trenton's first porcelain tableware form.

William Bloor (1821-1877) provided the spark needed for art porcelain production to begin in Trenton. Bloor worked first with James Taylor and Henry Speeler. He returned briefly to East Liverpool to begin his own firm; then, back in Trenton in 1863, he joined with Joseph Ott and Thomas Booth to produce ironstone in the newly built Etruria Pottery. (Booth later sold his

Facing page: Pitcher, yellow earthenware with brown, green, and blue glazes, circa 1854, height 10 inches. Taylor and Speeler (1852-ca. 1856) were advertised as "Manufacturers of all kinds of Porcelain, Queensware, Rockingham and Cane-Colored fireproof ware" in the city directory of 1854-1855. Although Taylor and Speeler's production of porcelain and queensware (a cream-colored earthenware perfected by Josiah Wedgwood in Staffordshire) has not been confirmed by extant samples, they certainly produced Rockingham of exceptional quality. (NJSM)

Above left: Commemorative pitcher, white ware, circa 1861, Millington, Astbury, and Poulson (1860-1865), height 9 inches. The pitcher shows Colonel Elmer E. Ellsworth, who was killed on August 24, 1861, as he descended the stairs of the Marshall House in Alexandria, Virginia, having removed a Confederate flag from the hotel's flagstaff. Richard Millington and John Astbury worked with William Young before building their pottery shop on Carroll Street. After 1878, Thomas Maddock took control of the works. Richard Millington operated the Albion House, a tavern popular with the English potters, for many years at Perry and Ewing streets. (NJSM)

Above: Pitcher, circa 1855, porcelain, William H. Young & Company (1853-1860), height 7 inches. Most of Young's production included commonplace items such as doorknobs, escutcheons, doorplates, and harness furniture. Young's pitchers in this pattern are considered to be Trenton's first porcelain tableware form. After 1860, the firm continued as William H. Young and Sons. Courtesy, NJSM, The Brewer Collection

interest to Garret Burroughs who in turn sold his interest to John Hart Brewer, Ott's nephew.) Before Bloor left the firm in 1871 they had produced at least two parian portrait busts (of Abraham Lincoln and Ulysses S. Grant), in addition to their regular crockery lines. Parian porcelain, named for its similarity to marble, is unglazed except for the interiors of pieces intended to hold liquid. Statuary is very effective in parian, though pitchers and vases were also made.

John Hart Brewer, having recently returned from a tour of duty in the Navy, was a young man eager for a future when he bought into the Etruria Pottery in 1864. Surely his brief association with Bloor had whetted his appetite for producing art porcelain.

In anticipation of this country's Centennial, Ott and Brewer hired Isaac Broome (1835-1922) to design several extraordinary parian pieces for display at the Exposition in Philadelphia in 1876. In addition to portrait busts of George Washington, Ulysses S. Grant, and others, Broome modeled the Baseball Vase, one of the finest examples of American 19th-century porcelain, and a bust of Cleopatra. For this bust he relied not on ancient depictions of the Egyptian queen but modeled his work on a Mrs. Thompson of Trenton.

Following the Centennial, Ott and Brewer continued to experiment with new porcelain formulas while maintaining their regular line of popular table and toilet wares in white ware. In 1883, they brought William Bromley, Sr. from Belleek, Ireland to achieve a true replication of the delicate Belleek porcelain. The porcelain developed in Belleek combined a thin translucent porcelain body, slip cast in extravagant shapes, with a pearly glaze invented in France. Skilled workmen from the Goss factory in Stoke-on-Trent, Staffordshire, were brought to Belleek to perfect the ware. William Bromley, Sr. was manager of these workmen.

Unfortunately, the best product does not always ensure prosperity. Business was good for Ott and Brewer's Etruria Pottery until 1892 when the combination of a long potters' strike and the depression of that same year forced them to close. In 1894 Brewer organized the Hart Brewer Pottery, which ceased production at his death in 1900. "I have labored for the success of our industry in a general way, and upon my own

Left: The "Baseball Vase," parian porcelain, 1876, designed by Isaac Broome (1835-1922) for the Ott and Brewer Company (1871-1892), height 32 inches. Made for display at the Centennial Exposition in Philadelphia, the Baseball Vase is one of the great monuments in American ceramic art. Isaac Broome already had a good reputation for work in architectural terra-cotta when Ott and Brewer hired him to design several sculptural pieces for their centennial display. Courtesy, NJSM, The Brewer Collection

Facing page top: Basket, 1883-1889, belleek porcelain, made by William Bromley, Sr., while working for the Ott and Brewer Company (1871-1892), length 8¼ inches. This basket attests to *the thorough knowledge and consummate skills that Bromley brought from Belleek, Ireland in 1883. Courtesy, NJSM, The Brewer Collection*

Facing page bottom: Workers in the glost kiln of the Dale and Davis Pottery (1880-1897) on Prospect Avenue pause for the camera in about 1890. Workers had to battle health conditions in potteries that were far more dangerous than many other industries of the time. Lung diseases, collectively called "potter's rot" but known today as chronic asthma and tuberculosis, were common because of poor ventilation in areas with high concentrations of dust. Dippers were contaminated with lead from the early glazes. (NJSM)

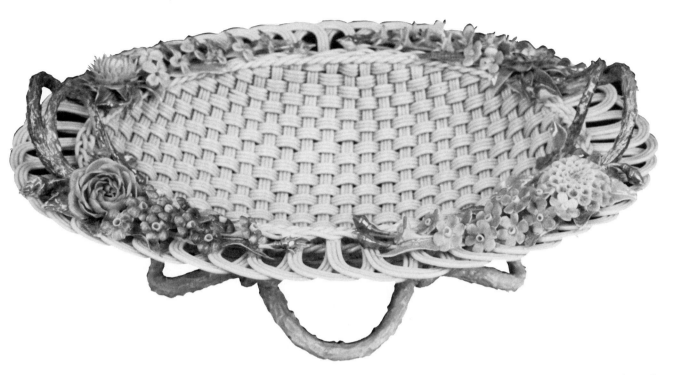

factory, for many years, and I am sorry to say that the reward, so far as profit is concerned, has been far from satisfactory," said Brewer. In his efforts for the industry he helped to organize the United States Potters' Association and the Trenton Potters' Association. As a member of Congress from 1880 to 1884 he served on the committees on accounts, railroads and canals, and manufactures. His principal work was for higher tariffs and the McKinley Tariff Act of 1890, which required foreign goods to be marked with the country of origin. Unfortunately, the Dingley Tariff Act, passed in 1897 during McKinley's administration, strengthened the American ceramic industry too late for Ott and Brewer to benefit.

In addition to Ott and Brewer's Etruria Pottery several other firms produced fine art porcelain beginning in the 19th century. The Greenwood Pottery Company was incorporated in 1868 out of Stephens, Tams & Company begun in 1862. The Tams family had emigrated from Staffordshire the year before. During the early years they made ironstone, but after 1876 specialized in vitrified hotel ware, electrical and telegraphic insulators, and porcelain hardware trimmings. This remarkably long-lived company survived until 1933 with these staple products as their mainstay. During the 1880s, the Tams family experimented with the manufacture of art porcelain which was marketed through such fine stores as Tiffany and Company in New York. Undoubtedly, economic considerations forced the company to discontinue the art line before 1890. The Tams' business survived for a much longer period of time than that of Ott and Brewer. Although both produced common wares as the backbone of their businesses, Ott and Brewer may have committed more energy toward experimentation and were perhaps less able financially to weather the severe economic storms of the 1890s.

The Willets Manufacturing Company began in 1879 in the works of William Young's Sons. The Willets brothers expanded this operation from four kilns to 13 large ware kilns and several smaller decorating kilns by 1890. Their mainstay was sanitary earthenware and white ironstone table and toilet wares, but they also made the fine creamy porcelain called belleek. In fact, they hired William Bromley, Sr. to develop it for them after he had perfected the process for Ott and Brewer. Unlike Ott and Brewer, the Willets' company survived until 1910, perhaps because they marketed much of their porcelain "in the white," without decoration.

The hand painting of porcelain requires a staff of skilled decorators if it is done in the factory. Although this provides a prestigious product for a pottery, the expense of employing decorators and of losing pieces

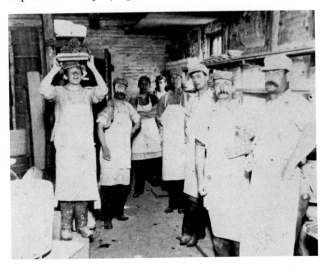

through successive firings can reduce profits enormously. Between 1880 and 1920 the fashion among middle and upper class women of leisure to paint on porcelain created a large market for undecorated porcelain. In addition to skilled factory decorators and amateur china painters there were studios which specialized in porcelain decoration in Trenton during this period. Chief among the studios clustered near North Clinton Avenue between Carroll and Mead streets were those of Samuel Sherratt and Jesse Dean. Independent decorators such as Peter Korzelius, who worked on the famous Trenton Vase for the St. Louis World's Fair of 1904, also found a ready market for their talents.

The most successful porcelain company in Trenton has been that founded by Walter Scott Lenox in 1889. As a boy Lenox was intrigued by the work in the Trenton potteries. Beginning at age 16 he served an apprenticeship with Isaac Davis. Lenox remembered when reflecting on this period, "All of the employees being English, I was not wanted there, so I offered my services for a year free." Later he worked for Ott and Brewer and the Willets Manufacturing Company. In 1889, at the age of 30, Lenox left Willets and went into partnership with Jonathon Coxon, Sr. (superintendent of Ott and Brewer's factory) as the Ceramic Art Company. Both believed that a company could survive on porcelain alone and did not need common crockery to stay in business.

The early years were not easy. Coxon withdrew in 1894 and in 1895 Lenox was stricken with a disease that left him blind as well as paralyzed in both legs. Despite his afflictions and against the advice of his creditors he kept the company going with the help of Harry Brown. In 1919 the company finally became solvent, and Lenox had a small model of a kiln built so he could smell the mortgage notes burn.

While decorative wares have continued to be made at Lenox, the real backbone of the company has been fine dinnerware in the same tradition as the English potteries. Quality control is extremely important in the fine dinnerware business, but marketing creates the buying public. The prestige Lenox sought came with the commission from President Woodrow Wilson in 1918 to produce the first American dinnerware to be used as the official White House service.

Despite economic cycles, labor problems, and the prominence of government as the major employer, Trenton is still the center of art porcelain production in the United States. Lenox, Inc. continues to produce the finest china dinnerware in America. Although the factory was moved to Pomona, New Jersey in the 1950s, the company maintains its corporate headquarters in the Trenton area.

The best studios for the production of porcelain figures are also in Trenton. The Polish artist Boleslaw Cybis began Cybis Porcelains in 1942. He had come to the United States in 1939 to paint frescoes in the Polish pavilion at the New York World's Fair and was prevented from returning to Poland by the German invasion. Before his death in 1957, he established the style that has carried forward to the present.

Edward Marshall Boehm, Inc., was founded in 1950. Boehm's love of animals and birds was expressed in his first profession, animal husbandry. His talent for art, however, led to his desire to produce birds, animals, and flowers in porcelain. By the time of his death in 1969, he had gathered together an able staff who continue today under the direction of Mrs. Helen Boehm. Art porcelain is the most difficult medium from which to profit financially. The fact that the industry continues to flourish in Trenton is a testament to the tradition begun by the pioneer porcelain makers as well as the continuity of native talent.

In considerations of American porcelain history little attention is paid to the contributions of the American sanitary ware makers to the rapid improvements made in health and hygiene during the last one hundred years. When Thomas Maddock arrived in New York City from Longport, England in 1847, he worked first as a porcelain decorator, the profession for which he was trained.

Facing page top: Workers finish greenware by sanding and sponging in the factory of Lenox, Inc., about 1923. Although millions of pieces of porcelain have been made in Trenton, each has received the careful hand finishing necessary for a superior product. (NJSM)

Lower left: Officers of the Greenwood Pottery Company (1868-1933) were photographed about 1890 in their showroom surrounded by the hotelware for which the company was famous. Finer wares may be seen in the cupboards through the doorway. James Tams is at the left. Courtesy, NJSM, Gift of Mrs. Arthur K. Twitchell in memory of her grandfather William Henry Tams and her father James Elmore Moffett Tams

Lower right: William H. Morley decorates a fish service for Lenox, Inc., about 1930. During his long career with Lenox from 1900 to 1934, Morley distinguished himself as a master of china decoration. He is most famous for his services with fish, game, orchids, and roses. Courtesy, Lenox, Inc.

He decided, however, that the development and manufacture of sanitary ware was the way to prosper in the American ceramic industry. In 1873 he joined the firm of Millington and Astbury who made a general line of white wares. Millington withdrew soon after. Maddock experimented in the manufacture of water closets and ignored Astbury's desire to make only crockery. In 1874 the factory first produced sanitary plumbing fixtures, thereby founding one of Trenton's major industries.

During the 1880s, all American ceramic bathroom fixtures were made in Trenton. Other firms were founded in Trenton because the technology already existed. By 1900, the importation of pottery plumbing fixtures from England, the other production center, had been reduced to a minimum. The American product was clearly better and the technology of sanitary ware continued to improve. Before the turn of the

century vitreous products were offered by many sanitary potteries.

During the early 20th century the industry in Trenton had become so specialized that smaller industries prospered in support of the sanitary ware makers. Moses Golding and his partners did a brisk business in grinding flint and feldspar, which took a dirty part of the process out of the potteries. Joseph Crossley specialized in the construction and maintenance of heavy equipment for the mixing and filtering of clays. Independent modelers, like "Big" John Kelly, were expert at making models from designers' requirements. Molds were made from these models and used in pressing and casting fixtures.

Plumbing fixtures were also made of enameled cast iron. Companies such as J.L. Mott of New York, Standard Sanitary of Pittsburgh, and the Kohler Company of Wisconsin were in competition for the same markets as the pottery manufacturers. Although enameled cast-iron water closets were clearly less desirable than those of pottery, wash basins were made of either material and bathtubs were usually enameled cast iron. Problems developed in the acquisition of larger orders forcing the pottery makers to cooperate with the iron manufacturers to fill big contracts. Beginning about 1920, the enameled cast-iron companies bought the potteries and assumed control of the whole industry.

The history of Thomas Maddock's Sons Company is typical. With prosperity seemingly assured the company built the most modern plant for pottery plumbing fixtures in existence in 1924-1925. The plant included the new Dressler tunnel kilns, which differed in both shape and performance from the traditional periodic kilns. Ware was loaded in the cold chamber of periodic kilns which was fired and then allowed to cool. The process took several days. A tunnel kiln is a continuous series of chambers through which a track runs. Greenware is loaded on open cars at one end and emerges fully fired from the other end the next day. The fires burn continuously; therefore a pottery can produce much more ware.

About the same time, however, the Kohler Company, with whom Maddock had cooperated on large orders, bought the Cochran-Dugan Company in Trenton and incorporated the pottery trade into their Wisconsin business. The Crane Company had already bought the Trenton Potteries Company. When the Maddock brothers approached American Radiator and Standard Sanitary to establish a cooperative agreement, Standard offered to buy out the Maddocks who agreed to sell in 1929. The American Standard Sanitary facility, still operating in Hamilton Township, has been greatly enlarged from the Maddocks' original plant.

The popularity of tiles in America paralleled the transition to indoor plumbing. Tiles in the bathroom provided a decoratively colored and patterned or pristine white hygienic surface for the walls and floors. In addition, tiles were used to embellish fireplaces and pave floors that received heavy traffic. Prior to 1880 tiles were not popular in America, but interest grew steadily until domestic production was valued at five million dollars annually in the years before World War I. Trenton's potteries shared in this enthusiasm for tiles.

The famous designers Isaac Broome and William Gallimore worked for the Trent Tile Company, which was in business from 1882 until 1938 and is now part of the Wenczel Tile Company still in the Trenton area. Broome founded the Providential Tile Works which operated from 1886 to 1913. Both companies were known for their high-glazed monochromatic pressed tiles with elegant designs in relief.

Herman Carl Mueller, a German potter, worked for the American Encaustic Tiling Company and founded the Mosaic Tile Company, both in Zanesville, Ohio, before organizing the Mueller Mosaic Company in Trenton in 1908. Until 1941, Mueller produced terra-cotta tiles with colorful matte glazes to be used inside and outside public and domestic buildings. Many of the installations designed by his company can still be seen in Trenton. The Crescent Temple is perhaps the most dramatic of these.

The ceramic industry in Trenton was much larger and far more complex than this brief history can suggest. Literally hundreds of big and small potteries operated from the 18th century to the present, but only a fraction have been mentioned to illustrate the general trends of the industry and emphasize important individuals. The many thousands of workers in these factories are the silent heroes of this chapter of Trenton's economic life.

Facing page: Tea set, belleek porcelain, 1893-1905, Morris & Willmore's Columbian Art Pottery (1893-1905), height 8¼ inches. W.T. Morris had worked at the Belleek works in Ireland, and both he and F.R. Willmore had worked for the Worcester Royal Porcelain Company in England (and for Ott and Brewer in Trenton) before forming the Columbian Art Pottery. (NJSM)

Above: Providential Tile Works and staff, circa 1895. Although the heavy work in potteries was done by men, there were many women and children employed in lighter tasks, particularly finishing, decorating, and packing. A Bureau of Labor Statistics report for New Jersey in 1894 noted that 30 percent of the workers in the pottery industry began work at the trade between 12 and 15 years of age. At the same time women accounted for 18 percent of the nearly 4,000 pottery workers in Trenton. Courtesy, Trentoniana Collection, TFPL

Right: "The Bride," 1980, porcelain, Cybis (1942-present), height 17¾ inches. Inspired by the painting of the same title executed by Boleslaw Cybis in 1937, "The Bride" was created in 1980 to commemorate the studio's 40th anniversary. The edition was limited to 100 examples. Courtesy, Cybis

Chapter Six

TRENTON AT THE TURN OF THE CENTURY

by Sam Graff and Sally Lane

The Battle Monument, whose corner-
stone had been laid on the 115th
anniversary of the Battle of Trenton,
was dedicated during elaborate
ceremonies October 19, 1893—the
112th anniversary of the surrender of
Cornwallis and the English army at
Yorktown. Note the flagpole sitter at
left. Courtesy, Trentoniana Collection, TFPL

*I*n 1876, when Trenton celebrated the 100th anniversary of the Hessians' defeat, it was a Protestant town that spoke English almost exclusively, a town that traveled in horsecars on unpaved streets, a town that was essentially the same place it had been before the Civil War.

Seventeen years later, when the monument marking the site of the First Battle of Trenton was dedicated in 1893, everything had changed. In the years from 1876 to 1893, the city's population had more than doubled, to 60,000. Most of the newcomers were foreign-born, and like their descendants to come, spoke languages other than English at home. Many of them were Catholic, as their descendants were to be, and almost all of them had been country people and longed like the suburbanites of the 1950s to break free from town and return to the soil they loved.

By 1905, when Trenton's population had reached 96,815, almost a third—28,442, according to the state census that year—couldn't speak English. Twenty-five years earlier, the 1880 federal census showed that the entire population of the city was only 29,910, and all, except for a handful of Germans, could speak the American language.

The face of the city also changed in those years. In 1870 the city demolished the market stalls that lined North Broad (then Greene) Street from State to Academy and moved the merchants and farmers down the street to the Washington Market, a kind of supermarket without carts, at South Broad and Front.

The city's two street railway companies, which had used horse power since they began running in 1863 and 1875, were combined under Col. Lewis Perrine in 1891. He electrified them the following year, reaching out to the new neighborhoods that were being thrown up to house the thousands of new potters and wire-pullers—and carpenters and bricklayers and masons—pouring into the city every year.

They built well, those Victorian craftsmen—so well that most of Trenton still lives in the comfortable brick houses they put up. Those homes line streets named for the men and ideals the 19th century revered: Cooper and Hewitt, Home and Centennial, Liberty and Union. A map of East Trenton is a history lesson in brick and asphalt, with streets named Lincoln and Grant, Jefferson and Kossuth, Sheridan and Perrine and Webster.

In Trenton, just about everybody who wanted a job had one, or at least a roof over his head. For most, it was work six days a week at the factory or on the railroad, to take home perhaps $60 a month.

It wasn't particularly easy at home for the wives of these workers, caring for what was usually a large brood of children and, often, boarders. The children went out to work as soon as they were able. The boys sold papers or learned a trade; the girls went to work as domestics, freeing other women to start such women's clubs as the Contemporary, founded in 1897.

For most of the men, the work was dirty and dangerous. There was no Occupational Safety and Health Administration in those days, and losing fingers and hands was all part of the job in the wire mills. As for railroading, we can get some idea of the hazards of that work from the *Railroad Trainmen's Journal.* The inside back cover of the June 1903 issue, for example, carries a full-page ad for the Winkley Artificial Limb Co. of Minneapolis ("Warranted not to chafe the stump"). Inside, there was a list of those seeking death and permanent disability benefits. Among the 80 names listed that month is that of William R. Howell, a member of Trenton Lodge No. 38, Brotherhood of Railroad Trainmen, made up of Reading Railroad brakemen. On April 29, 1903, the magazine laconically notes, he "fell between cars; run over" and died.

They were hard-working people, those unskilled laborers whose work endures, and they were hard praying, hard playing, and hard drinking as well. *Fitzgerald's City Directory* for 1886-1887, for example, lists 37 churches and two solid pages of saloons. In 1910, the *Trenton Manual* lists 97 churches—and 293 saloons.

But even with all those taverns, and the hundreds of social clubs and fraternal groups—including 19 lodges of Free & Accepted Masons, 18 lodges of International Order of Odd Fellows, and 32 Catholic societies in 1900 alone—singing societies, military units, veterans' organizations, yes, and even gambling clubs to tempt the honest working man, it wasn't all beer and skittles. Closing time in the saloons was 11 p.m., music and floor shows had to stop by 9:30 p.m. (except on Saturdays) and bars were closed on Sundays all day.

The stringent saloon rules—the result of the work of the largely Methodist Women's Christian Temperance Union and the three Catholic total-abstinence leagues—may have been one reason why so many social clubs existed. As long-time newspaperman and bon vivant George Shick recalled in the *Trenton Times* in 1963, "Oldtimers wink when asked how strictly the Sunday closing and clamp on entertainment were observed. Pri-

vate clubs flourished . . . where a drink could be had and a game of cards enjoyed when saloons were closed."

Trenton apparently has been a gambling town ever since William Trent decided to take a chance on putting his plantation on the south side of the Assunpink Creek. But, as John J. Cleary's *Sunday Times-Advertiser* column, "Trenton in Bygone Days," reported in 1936, "the turn of the century ushered in the Golden Age of gambling. One of the best known outposts was the Peerless Club . . ." eventually headquartered on Hudson (then Jenny) Street, between Genesee and Clinton, in the shadow of the Roebling plant. The members had a craps table "that would accommodate from 40 to 50 players" and hired a New Yorker identified only as English Tommy to run it for them for a cut of five percent. "After a few years," the column reports, Tommy ". . . left Trenton, taking along with him $200,000."

There were two popular trotting tracks in that era, both along Pennington Road. The Ewing Track was behind the Cross Keys Tavern at the northeast corner of Ewingville Road. The other half-mile oval, the Trenton Driving Park, opened in 1892 at Scotch Road and the following year was host to a stallion named Nelson, who set a world's record at 2:11-1/4. And the Interstate Fair, which moved to Nottingham Way in 1888, attracted crowds of up to 100,000 for its annual race meetings.

People even bet on other people. The *Daily True American* of October 18, 1893 reports, "A foot race will take place at Hill's Grove next Monday between Fred Schultz, of Trenton, and Frank Robinson, of Tullytown, for $50 a side."

Trentonians liked speed of any kind. There were so many bicyclists in the city by 1905 that the police organized a special bicycle force to keep riders from

knocking over pedestrians.

Then the auto arrived, soon followed by the Trenton-made Mercer and its dirt-track testing in Hamilton Township. The Interstate Fair added auto races in 1900, and cars were so popular that even as late as 1910 a crowd would gather at State and Broad whenever one stopped.

There were team sports, too. Baseball replaced cricket in those days, just as in the fall soccer replaced rugby and football eventually replaced them both—except in the hearts of Trentonians just off the boat.

Indoors in winter, there was basketball (in fact, the world's first professional basketball game was played in 1896 in Trenton) and outdoors there was skating and ice-boating on the Delaware and on the canals.

The water was the place to be in summer, too. A half-dozen canoe clubs flourished, yacht clubs beckoned, and for many a Trenton youngster, a ride to Philadelphia on a steamboat (fare 25 cents) was the high point of the summer.

There were no television sets or movies, but there was Taylor's Opera House and, after the turn of the century, the State Street and Trent theaters as well. A list of stars who appeared there reads like a theatrical Who's Who: John Drew, Dion Boccicault, Ethel and John Barrymore, Lillian Russell, Sarah Bernhardt, Lillie Langtry, Victor Herbert, Tyrone Power, Sr., Madame Modjeska and Trenton's own Rose Stahl and Ruth Donnelly.

Facing page: In late June of 1898, when the national convention of the Ancient Order of Hibernians came to town, this arch welcomed them at South Warren near State Street. Twenty-eight feet wide and 26 feet high, the arch made ample use of electric lights, which outlined WELCOME and AOH in crimson. The platform above the arch housed Winkler's Band for nightly concerts. Courtesy, Trentoniana Collection, TFPL

Above: The Union Fire Company, founded in February of 1747, was Trenton's first volunteer unit. When the city's 13 volunteer companies were disbanded 145 years later, the whole city turned out for the parade on Monday, April 4, 1892, at 2:00 in the afternoon. The school board shut schools at noon, and the mayor asked all factories and stores to close. With thousands of spectators lining the streets in the 78-degree weather—the hottest for that date in 20 years—1,000 volunteers marched. The American Hose Company at Perry and Ewing streets became Engine 6 at midnight, when the city's paid fire department was inaugurated. Courtesy, Trentoniana Collection, TFPL

Prosperous families had pianos and phonographs; there were all those clubs to join and sports to play.

Those were boom years for Trenton, but years when Trentonians had to fight to get ahead. A dispute in 1883 brought two newsboys into court. Morris Makelsky of 22 Market Street and Louis Berger of South Warren Street were arrested at State and Broad after Louis hit Morris when he complained that Louis was stealing his customers. "Ain't I got a right to sell papers as well as him?" Louis asked the judge. His Honor agreed, but when Louis' father couldn't pay his $1 fine, locked him up anyway.

Trenton has often been a tough place for the small businessman.

Far left, top: Forty years after the Civil War ended, the 38th Encampment of New Jersey's Grand Army of the Republic brought the state's surviving veterans to Trenton on Thursday, June 22, 1905. As they marched past City Hall at State and Broad, the photographer snapped local men he knew: drummer Benjamin McClurg, James Clugston (behind the flag-bearer), and James Gordon on the right. Courtesy, Sally Lane

Far left, bottom: The photographer of this 1898 group portrait labeled it "Miss Margerum's birthday party at Hotel Windsor." Opened in 1883, the hotel occupied a pair of four-story brownstones on East State Street. Courtesy, Sally Lane

Left, top: The first of the city's street railways, the Trenton Horse Railroad Company was chartered by the legislature in 1859. Cars were not to run on Sunday, the fare was to be five cents, and the speed of the one-horse cars was not to exceed six miles per hour. In

1883, when this picture was taken, six cars were in constant operation, running at eight-minute intervals along the route from the sheds opposite Charles G. Roebling's house on West State Street to the Clinton Street Station. Courtesy, Trentoniana Collection, TFPL

Left, bottom: Beginning in 1894, Peter Curtin manned his lunch wagon outside City Hall at State and Broad every night for 17 years — the sole exception being the night Broad Street was paved. Arriving at 8:30, he'd sell food and drink until 4:30. Most sandwiches were a nickel, but both ham and eggs and chicken were a dime. Coffee and milk were a nickel each, and business was so good that Curtin bought a dairy farm. His trade picked up each night around 11:00 when the saloons closed, and people gathered at State and Broad for the final trolley run. The side of his wagon shows an amusing version of Columbus' discovery of America. Courtesy, Trentoniana Collection, TFPL

Facing page top: Crisp's Fish Cars sold "Fresh Ocean Fish, Clams & Oysters Retailed at Wholesale Prices," as the painted wagons photographed here in 1899 proclaim. The oyster cracker business was born on Centre Street in 1847. English baker Adam Exton used just three ingredients—wheat flour, vegetable shortening, and salt—but by the turn of the century his "Trenton crackers" had 30 imitators. Courtesy, Trentoniana Collection, TFPL

Facing page bottom: The Trenton Canoe Club, the city's first, was formed in 1884, followed by the Mohawk, West End, Chippewa, Algonquin, Hiawatha, and Park Island groups, among others. This later 1880s photo shows members of the Algonquin Club standing outside their handsome clubhouse at low tide. Canoeists for the most part used the river above the State House, while yachting enthusiasts used the Lalor Street dock. Courtesy, Trentoniana Collection, TFPL

Top: By the late 1880s, when cycling was all the rage among their elders, children decorated their bicycles for parades, like this one along Greenwood Avenue. By June of 1893 the first night of cycle racing under electric lights took place. The height of the local craze came at noon on June 24, 1896; seated on their bicycles outside the bride's Lamberton Street home, Harry E. Stahl and Nettie Morris were married in their cycling costumes. After the ceremony, the couple pedaled away to a New York State honeymoon, including a visit to

Niagara Falls. Courtesy, Trentoniana Collection, TFPL

Above: Following its incorporation on July 22, 1889, the Park Island Canoeing Association bought White's Island, renaming it Park Island, and built its clubhouse there that same year. This 1890s view of the group's island camp includes a small boy dressed in a Little Lord Fauntleroy outfit perched on a tent pole. Courtesy, Trentoniana Collection, TFPL

Far left, top: The city's first skyscraper, the Broad Street National Bank, was built on the southwest corner of East State and Montgomery streets in 1900. The first city building to be constructed with a modern steel framework and the first to rise more than four stories (eight floors at first, later expanded to 12), the bank captured the public imagination. From its roof, intrepid visitors had a panoramic view of the city. The less adventurous could avail themselves of the town's first revolving doors at the street level. Courtesy, Trentoniana Collection, TFPL

Near left, top: The first City Hall was built in 1837 on the northeast corner of Broad and State (Greene and Second) streets and reflected urban prosperity more suitably than the former Town Hall on Academy Street. The building housed the offices of the mayor, the common council, and the police and served as the local jail. This view shows its appearance in 1891 after Victorian remodeling. It still stands as a commercial building. Courtesy, Trentoniana Collection, TFPL

Facing page bottom: The Trenton High School football team of 1897-1898: front row, Alfred P.S. Bellis, Bentley H. Pope, Arthur Atwood; middle row, S. Nori, Lee D. Hirsch, Theodore Tobish, Amos Penrose, Duane Green; back row, Theodore Myers, Matthew J. Scammell, Morris Van Horn, and Andrew Wren. Courtesy, Trentoniana Collection, TFPL

Right: The city's oldest house, built in 1719 by William Trent, wore all the trappings of Victorian design and two new wings by the turn of the century. This Turkish corner, the height of late Victorian extravagance, was complete down to the water pipe, fans, and tented bed. When Edward Ansley Stokes gave his family home to the city in 1929, this part of the house was razed in the restoration. Courtesy, William Trent House

Below: Throughout Trenton's history the city streets have been prone to flooding because of the low elevation of the river plain. This 1903 Venetian scene on South Warren Street is typical of floods that have occurred for over three centuries. Courtesy, Trentoniana Collection, TFPL

Chapter Seven

BETWEEN THE WARS

For two years Woodrow Wilson was a reform-oriented New Jersey governor. This photograph shows the future President leaving the State House after his 1910 inaugural ceremony. He was elected to the White House in 1912. Courtesy, Trentoniana Collection, TFPL

By 1917 Trenton would never again be called "a pretty village" or a languishing country town, for the factories had irrevocably altered the face of the city and its skyline. It rightly earned inclusion in a recent book on gritty cities, and housekeepers in East Trenton can still vouch for the air that carries the unmistakable evidence of the nearby presence of manufacturing plants.

In the fall of 1910, Woodrow Wilson left the life of a Princeton University professor and college president when he came to the New Jersey governor's office in Trenton to learn the art of politics. He took his recently earned reputation as a successful progressive administrator from the State House to the White House in less than three years with the ardent support of *Trenton Times* editor-owner James Kerney, who wrote of his years as the governor's confidant in the book *The Political Education of Woodrow Wilson*.

Wilson won re-election to the American presidency in 1916 by campaigning under the slogan "he kept us out of war." But within a few weeks of his second inaugural on March 5, 1917, the society pages of the Trenton papers featured the area's first naval and first army bride of the impending war. Headlines announcing the Germans' intention to begin unrestricted submarine warfare warned local reservists and National Guards that American involvement was imminent. The first troops to be mobilized in Trenton on March 28, 1917 were in the Second Regiment of the National Guard. Wilson called Congress into extraordinary session and delivered an eloquent apologia for declaration of war against Germany to the Joint Houses on April 2.

With the official declaration on April 6, Trenton's industries had to cope with increased demand for new materials coupled with the depletion of the work force by enlistments, military draft, and restricted immigration. Restrictive regulations applying to major ports limited the activities of industries producing civilian goods in order to stimulate the national defense effort. Women, never before publicly encouraged to work in lumber yards, banks, or heavy-industry factories, would appear in those facilities "just for the duration." Their sacrifice in the cause of a war to end all wars was the impelling reason for the successful adoption of the 19th Amendment, which granted New Jersey women suffrage again after a hiatus of over a century, in 1920.

With a large foreign-born population, the city's ethnic communities were, by the 20th century's early decades, easily identifiable, despite the pervasive efforts at Americanization practiced by the schools, the citizenship process, and the press. In 1910, 27 percent of the city's population, then 96,815, was foreign born, and of those 3,968 (about 15 percent) were German. Within a decade, the city's population of 119,289 was 25 percent foreign born with a decrease to 2,338 in the number of those born in Germany. The city's first foreign-language newspaper was the *New Jersey-Staats-Journal* founded in 1867, which continued as a weekly until the Second World War.

By the onset of World War I, the German character of Chambersburg was being replaced by the swelling wave of Italian immigrants. The popular annual harvest festival, a German tradition begun in 1886, was discontinued after almost 30 years, but the German singing societies, such as the East Trenton Mannerchor, continued by merging with the Trenton Liedertafel.

The 5,200 Trenton area men in the active fighting services and the uncounted numbers of men and women in the auxiliary services returned home to parades, receptions, and a housing shortage. The war nonetheless engendered a civic spirit that gave birth to more than a decade of city boosterism. The pro-Trenton spirit was most likely a course pursued by city leaders to unite the separate ethnic neighborhoods and to develop a sense of an American community among so many nationalities.

One of the more visible manifestations of this spirit is the magnificent War Memorial Building, erected with a $423,000 contribution raised by the community in a fund drive. The state donated the thousands of dollars given by its school children for a New Jersey memorial immediately after the close of the war. The city and the county each appropriated $200,000 to what was originally thought of as a peace memorial—a large civic auditorium between the State House and the Delaware River. It was completed in 1932 having been ten years in the planning stage.

The decade 1919 to 1929 was also a time of numerous community achievements, from a Presidential visit to the installation of a lighted city slogan that spanned the new highway bridge over the Delaware.

Typical of the era's positive community spirit was the 1919 formation of the Trenton Historical Society, which recorded two noteworthy events in its first 10 years of existence. On December 29, 1926, President Calvin Coolidge accepted the Society's invitation to take part in a celebration of the 150th anniversary of the First Battle of Trenton. Coolidge, his wife Grace Anna, and their

party took over an entire floor of the five-year-old Stacy-Trent Hotel. Coolidge's address before the all-male Society, as described in the *Trenton Times,* "was delivered before probably the most brilliant assemblage ever gathered here." The evening's proceedings were broadcast live by radio station WOR, and motion pictures of the event were shown in local theaters.

The previously mentioned Stacy-Trent Hotel was built by public subscription at the instigation of the Rotary Club and the Chamber of Commerce. Its purpose was to attract conventions to Trenton with a large modern facility to complement the state capital's other attractions. The hotel remained a landmark in the city's life for half a century, surviving by renting out suites of offices and rooms for a few state officials. Its site was finally pre-empted for a new office building to house the State Department of the Treasury.

In 1928 the County Board of Chosen Freeholders issued *A Sketch of Mercer County New Jersey 1838-1928*

Above: After a fire in 1885 the front section of the State House was rebuilt and enlarged in the Renaissance style, and the dome was raised in height. This view shows a portion of the 1792 structure on the right behind the new facade. Courtesy, Trentoniana Collection, TFPL

Facing page top left: Trenton's War Memorial Building honored the soldiers, sailors, and airmen who gave their lives in World War I. For many years operas, plays, graduation ceremonies, civic occasions, and the concerts of the Trenton Symphony Orchestra have taken place in its capacious theater.

Facing page top right: This view shows the Sacred Heart Church soon after it was built in 1899. It stands on the site of St. John's Church, the oldest Roman Catholic parish in New Jersey. The rectory stands to the right of the church. For many years the church's Catholic Club was a center for literary, musical, and sporting activities. Courtesy, Trentoniana Collection, TFPL

Facing page bottom: A line of cavalrymen is seen advancing on West State Street toward the city center as part of the parade held in November 1926 to honor the 150th anniversary of the First Battle of Trenton. For the past two centuries parades have often commemorated Trenton's role in the Revolutionary War. Courtesy, Trentoniana Collection, TFPL

which exemplifies the community promotion so prevalent in all public descriptions of the area. No modesty here: the Foreword states that the booklet hopes to present an accurate picture of the county, but that it will be "painted in bold strokes" to create "a pride of home." In heavy type, the committee advertises that taxes have been kept among the lowest in the state by a progressive and patriotic citizenry. On the page devoted to population an astute reader will discover that by 1925 the number of black people in Mercer County (6,991) exceeded the farm population (6,037). The city of Trenton claimed 76 percent of the county's population with Hamilton Township a far distant 9 percent as the most populous suburb.

Under transportation, statistics are interspersed between photographs of the recently established Mercer County airport—"the final touch of modernness to the already more than ample" facilities. To eyes accustomed to multi-level terminals and jumbo jets, the airport appears to be an open, treeless, grassy field with a large crowd of people almost inundating the three tiny planes. But the airport's 140 acres offered a flat tract with a powerful beacon light, and it had already been designated as the official United States intermediate landing field for the New York-to-Atlanta aerial mail route. It was, according to *A Sketch of Mercer County*, "a forward looking step taken by the Mercer Board of Freeholders." Land transport was also possible via the 72 miles of electric trolley lines. In addition, the city's 500 industrial establishments were served by 42 miles of sidings connected to the main lines of the Pennsylvania or the Reading Railroad.

Also bringing 20th-century technology to Trenton

Above: The lower Trenton-Morrisville Bridge is near the site of a colonial ferry crossing. The first bridge across the Delaware was built here in 1806, but that wooden bridge was replaced by an iron structure in 1876. The present bridge opened in 1929 and has become a familiar city symbol because of its sign "Trenton Makes, the World Takes." The slogan was chosen from among entries in a 1910 contest.

Facing page: The present First Methodist Church on South Broad Street, built in 1894, stands on the site of an 1838 church. Its tower is a familiar landmark. In 1929 a capacity crowd gathered at the church to hear a lecture on "250 Years of History" as part of the city's 250th anniversary.

was the establishment of radio station WOAX in 1923. In the 1940s the call letters were changed to WTNJ, then in the 1960s to WAAT, to WTNJ in 1972, and, since 1979, the station has been on the air as WIMG, making it one of the nation's oldest continuously broadcasting radio stations. It is one of 10 commercial stations serving the area, along with a number of local college radio stations.

Patriotic occasions have long been celebrated by the citizenry of Trenton, and with the conclusion of the First World War, such celebrations came to occupy a prominent role in the civic life of the area. In 1920 the Trenton Teachers' Club presented a pageant at the Grand Theatre on December 15 and 16, commemorating the Tercentenary of the Landing of the Pilgrims with an event titled "The Lighting of the Torch." On Flag Day, 1927, a civic event was held in the Armory to celebrate the 150th anniversary of the adoption of the Star Spangled Banner. These programs involved a variety of ethnic and religious groups in an attempt to reinforce their "Americanism," in contrast to the 1893 celebration of Washington's Birthday in which red ribbons

proclaimed the sponsors as the "American Secret Societies and Public School Children of Trenton."

When the George Washington Bicentennial came in 1932, the local committee compiled a descriptive booklet emphasizing a variety of commemorative activities to involve all school children, the Trenton Historical Society, and a number of commercial establishments. There was an official course of study and a bibliography of appropriate readings, demonstrating an informative approach rather than mere emotional appeals to nationalism. Of course that aspect wasn't entirely neglected but evidently it took second place.

Between the 1926 sesquicentennial of the Battles of Trenton and the George Washington Bicentennial occurred the strictly local celebration of the 250th anniversary of the settlement of Trenton in 1929. It was, by far, the largest and most festive commemoration in Trenton and has probably not been equalled since. It featured a historical program by the Reverend Hamilton Schuyler, a local history writer who wrote and directed the event's pageant. A civic hymn, "Trenton-on-the-Delaware," was set to music by Paul Ambrose. The sixth

verse of the song, as published in *The Trenton Sunday-Times Advertiser*, typifies the mood of the celebration:

Artisan and craftsman cunning
In the busy shop and mill
Many useful wares producing
By their industry and skill,
Spread abroad the city's name,
Bring to Trenton wealth and fame.
City of our pride and care,
Trenton on the Delaware!

The official program of the Trenton settlement celebration appears in the October issue of *Trenton Magazine*, the house organ of the city's Chamber of Commerce. The magazine had been started in July 1924 as "a constructive monthly review of people, facts and events which are making for a greater and better Trenton." For 25 cents local people could purchase the October issue, which contained numerous photographs, including 14 aerial views of the city, and a detailed description of the week's activities from October 27 to November 2.

On Saturday, October 26, as a preliminary to the week's program, an air show was presented as part of the dedication of the Mercer Airport facilities. The crowd was estimated at between 20,000 to 35,000 people, and one reporter stated that it was safe to say that every boy in Trenton who could possibly get away was at the airport, along with the governor, county dignitaries, and an army pilot, Lieutenant James Doolittle.

The week's official activities began on Sunday the 27th as Religious Day. Trenton's churches were encouraged to hold special services with historic themes, and in the afternoon a choral service of nearly 300 voices was scheduled to be held in Cadwalader Park. The November celebration review issue of the *Trenton Magazine* stated that the brisk air that Sunday was not ideal for vocal chords, so the service was held at the Lincoln Theatre. In the evening there was an overflow meeting at the First Methodist Church to hear a Princeton University professor lecture on "250 Years of History."

Monday was declared Civic Day and was celebrated with a colorful parade of policemen, firemen, and city employees, as well as welfare, fraternal, and civic organizations in uniforms and marching units. A parade of 20,000 school children and young men and women in "higher institutions of learning" marked the Tuesday

observance of Education Day. It was considered a great spectacle to see the children from every city public, parochial, and business school, the Teachers College, and from the three bordering townships parading through the streets in costumes, uniforms, or on floats. (That date is remembered in history books, however, as "Black Tuesday" when the stock market fell so dramatically, presaging the Great Depression.)

Wednesday was Historic Day. The morning featured a pilgrimage to historic places in and around Trenton, and Wednesday night brought the Historical Society's banquet marked by the usual oratory. It was a joyous addition to the commemorative events when Edward Ainsley Stokes of Morristown gave the city the gift of Bloomsbury Court, with the stipulation that the house be restored to its original state.

Ladies' Day was held on Thursday and was celebrated with a Colonial Tea in the afternoon at the Old Barracks and a Colonial Costume Ball attended by about 300 guests at the Stacy-Trent Hotel Ballroom that evening. These were the era's typical social activities for the "fairer sex." There were signs of changing times, however, in the female bylines which accompanied several articles in the October and November issues of the Chamber of Commerce magazine.

Professional women were beginning to assume influential roles in the public sphere, and the ladies of the community were learning the value and power of organization. Their first effort was the Contemporary Club, founded in 1897. In addition to its outstanding work with social services, such as the establishment of

the Carolyn Stokes Day Nursery, the Contemporary Club continues to attract "doers" among the area's women by incorporating the issues of the day into their community work. The Trenton College Club, founded in 1911, the Business and Professional Women's Club (1916), and the Junior League (1921) have been augmented more recently by Zonta, the Soroptimists, and various black sororities which influence the quality of life for the betterment of all women in the community.

For many Trentonians, the 1929 celebration of the city's founding is vividly remembered for its parades. The city closed its stores, schools, and industries on Friday afternoon so that employees and youngsters could join the thousands of visitors crowding the curbs, upper-story windows, and rooftops on that beautiful November afternoon. There were some 51 floats or processions of costumed re-enactors portraying important events in the history of the city, local institutions and industries, and 11 European nations. The event was so picturesque that the Sunday *New York Times* carried photographs of it.

All New Jersey was represented in the Volunteer Firemen's Parade on Saturday afternoon. Despite the rain, onlookers lined the exceptionally long route from Prospect Street to the Fairgrounds in Hamilton Township. They cheered the various fire-fighting units as they shook surplus water from their hats, smiling even though they were soaking wet. The miles of riverfront provided the setting for the other Saturday afternoon attraction, a four-hour regatta. There was a one-and-a-half mile speedboat course "from the old brewery to the railroad bridge now under construction," and a luncheon on a barge donated by the Delaware River Navigation Company. But the center of the general swirl of the hubbub along the waterfront was the Trenton Yacht Club.

By the 1920s the waterfront was drawing the attention of civic activists for commercial and recreational development. Under the persistent vision of General Wilbur F. Sadler (president of the Broad Street Bank) Stacy Park was created from the marshland behind the State House. This gave the city a downtown green sward to surround the state buildings and the historic 18th century buildings of the Old Barracks and the Old Masonic Lodge, which had been recently restored in the early decades of the 20th century.

Complementing Stacy Park was the Trenton Marine Terminal, specially built for industrial development along the waterfront on the city's border with Hamilton Township. The key to making Trenton a major port was assuring a sufficiently deep channel upriver from Philadelphia. A turning basin was created at the Trenton Municipal Wharf. By 1932, the river depth was 25 feet at mean low water so that ships could dock with a weight load as high as 15,000 tons.

Trenton's other waterfront—the Delaware and Raritan Canal—was being manipulated into extinction by its owner/competitor, the Pennsylvania Railroad. From the time of its purchase by the railroad at the end of the 19th century, use of the canal declined sharply until the last commercial vessel traversed it in 1932. Industrialists thought there was no reason to mourn the loss of the waterway which had united Trenton with

Facing page top: In October 1929 Trenton marked its 250th anniversary with a week of festivities. Tuesday, October 29, was Education Day, and uniformed children from every school in the region marched through the downtown streets. Here a young bugle corps passes in review. Courtesy, Trentoniana Collection, TFPL

Facing page bottom: On Historic Day, during Trenton's 250th anniversary, horse-drawn floats depicted notable events of the past. The Italian-American Columbus float, seen in this view at State and Broad streets, was judged as

the finest in the parade. Courtesy, Trentoniana Collection, TFPL

Above: The Carolyn Stokes Day Nursery was founded by the social service department of the Contemporary Club in 1924. Located in the East Trenton industrial section, its trained staff provides free clinics, family advising, and a boys' club. Members of the Contemporary Club join the children in saying grace in this 1957 photograph. Courtesy, Trentoniana Collection, TFPL

Lambertville by the 22-mile long Canal Feeder—and New Brunswick by the 42-mile length from Bordentown—because both the Reading and the Pennsylvania railroads had major installations in Trenton. The canal was left to a few fishermen, wintertime skaters, and daring youngsters anxious for a swim on a hot summer's day. The Mercer County Master Plan of 1931 considered the canal extremely picturesque and rich in recreational opportunities, and planners believed that in such an intensively developed region as Trenton, especially in the downtown section, the canal could offer a waterway park at little expense.

But the final disposition of the canal was more prosaic. The empty canal bed became the Trenton Freeway, permitting the automobile to skirt the industrial areas of East Trenton. The canal was filled in, the water diverted into underground culverts for industrial use, and a six-mile, four-lane highway was constructed after the Works

Progress Administration drained and filled in the canal bed locally in 1936. Traffic could then leave the downtown commercial district, unhindered by traffic lights, to spill out onto the less populated Hamilton and Lawrence townships.

Another victim of the emergence of the automobile was the electric railway, popularly referred to as the trolley. Although there was half-hourly service between Trenton and Camden, the line could not compete successfully with the paralleling Pennsylvania Railroad for speed-conscious commuters and generally depended on thrifty local travellers. The city street railway system had been electrified in 1892 after being horse-drawn since its beginnings in 1863. Despite an almost unbelievable variation of track gauges, the lines spread out like crows' feet to the surrounding villages by the turn of the century. Bordentown, Yardville, Hamilton Square, Lawrenceville, Princeton, Pennington, and Hopewell were all then easily accessible to the central city to regular commuters.

Travel to communities south along the Delaware was instituted with the Trenton-to-Camden line. By 1923 the trolleys also had to compete with buses which were not saddled with rail maintenance costs. Ten years later, the Trenton Transit Company went into receivership. On December 28, 1934, its power was turned off at 3:00 p.m., and its equipment sold. The Perry Street terminal building, though used for other purposes, still bears the incised words "motor coach" and "trolley,"

Above: Before the advent of the automobile, the interurban trolley was popular for daily commuting, shopping, or a weekend ride. The trolleys of the Trenton Street Railway Company linked the city with the nearby townships from 1892 to 1934. Courtesy, Trentoniana Collection, TFPL

Facing page: A picket line of unemployed workers marched in front of the State House in 1935 to plead for jobs at a union wage or relief at a living standard. The employment situation did not improve locally until the national economy began to revive in the late 1930s. Courtesy, The Trenton Times

and the open paved yard tells a story of public transportation that shaped the physical dimensions of the area.

Other traces of the trolleys were systematically removed. But the observant walker in Trenton will occasionally spot a portion of the shiny rail where a more recently laid street surface has worn thin. Many of the seemingly aimless open avenues of the Public Service Right of Way are vestiges of the trolleys' abandoned traction lines. The county bus service of the 1980s, Mercer Metro, is the transformed Trenton Transit Company, which is a private business that was formed after lengthy negotiations that resulted in the merging of a number of traction companies.

The exaggeration engendered by the boosterism of the Roaring Twenties is apparent in the 1930 census figures. Trenton's promotional literature estimated the city population at 136,000 in 1927, and by including the immediately adjacent built-up sections just beyond the city line, 170,000 people. But in reality the city's 1930 population, according to the U.S. Census, was 123,356. Over 19 percent of the population was European born

and 6.4 percent (8,057) was described as Negro. The population had actually grown less in a decade than it had in little more than one year in the period from 1910 to 1920 when the average annual population increase was 3,422 people. Of the county's 1930 census total— 187,143—the city's population represented only 66 percent; this was a 10 percent *decrease* from the comparable figures for 1920. And yet statistics indicate that the three adjacent townships to the city were actually doubling their population in a decade. Although the actual township populations were only a small fraction of the city's, more attention should have been paid to the reasons why Ewing Township grew from 3,475 to 6,942; Hamilton from 14,580 to 27,121; and Lawrence from 3,686 to 6,293. Indeed, both Ewing and Hamilton had previously doubled their populations in the decade from 1910 to 1920.

Hindsight makes it easy now to point out that this was the beginning of the flight to the suburbs. City leaders, oblivious to the meaning of these statistics, continued to glow with pride about the first-class status of their municipality. What neighboring township had a park and zoo designed by Frederick Olmsted; a riverfront dotted with colonial structures; hundreds of varied industries; the state and county seat of government; bakeshops and restaurants serving a number of ethnic tastes; a reservoir and a sewage system? No, they thought, Trenton is the only place to live; who would want to buy a house in the suburbs when they could buy a city property with all the

amenities? They ignored the appeal of lower land costs, and lower taxes, and the free or inexpensive use of the city's facilities by suburbanites who wanted to take advantage of such benefits as the public library.

Suburban growth was temporarily forestalled, however, by the terrible economic conditions of the next decade's depression. In a 1937 federal census the figures show that the chief breadwinner was unemployed in between 35 and 45 percent of the city's families. Fewer women than men were out of work, but of course a much smaller percentage of women had regular jobs. Still, among the black population, it was more likely that a black woman would find domestic work than a black man would find a job.

Trentonians, still in the grip of the Depression's unemployment, had occasion to rejoice when General Motors announced on June 17, 1937, that it had purchased an 83-acre tract on Parkway Avenue in Ewing Township. Two months later, the governor of New Jersey, Harold G. Hoffman, turned the first shovel of dirt for the first plant built outside the Detroit area to produce GM's ternstedt products—primarily hardware. In November 1938 nearly 600 government, civic, business, and industrial leaders gathered at the Stacy-Trent Hotel for a celebration luncheon when the six-million-dollar plant officially opened its door to the "great day . . . great event" speeches of the Chamber of Commerce officials. And local workers, who had been glad to get a job averaging 14 cents an hour, swamped the GM employment office for places on the assembly line at a wage scale of 24 to 89 cents per hour. By 1941, the plant's payroll reached 5.1 million dollars.

The nation's entry into World War II also changed the industrial tempo of the Delaware Valley. Ewing's GM plant closed in mid-December to reopen under a new name—the Eastern Aircraft Division—and the assembly line was revamped to build, not cars, but Grumman TBF Avenger torpedo bombers for Navy aircraft carriers. The two-front war required a round-the-clock, seven-day-a-week operation and the plant employed some 15,000 people to turn out eight Avengers per day. Housewives who had never worked outside their homes, high school students on summer vacation, black domestic workers, and practically anyone wishing to work was wanted and desperately needed. Though the frenetic pace of wartime production eventually came to a close, the war brought profound and lasting changes to Trenton's social fabric, as thousands of blacks and women entered the mainstream of the city's well-paying industrial work force, raising expectations about their lifestyle.

Today nostalgia plays many tricks with the memories of Trentonians but there was a tremendous appeal and excitement to life in Trenton in the decades between the wars. Many old-time residents look back on those years and describe the friendly, comfortable atmosphere of the community. People from scores of miles away in central New Jersey and eastern Pennsylvania came to Trenton for shopping and entertainment. The secret of this attraction was that Trenton was an overgrown small town where stores had a reputation for friendly, personal service and cultural offerings reflected the provincial taste of rural America. Despite its claim to be a first-class city, Trenton was still a community of ethnic neighborhoods and surrounding homogenous villages.

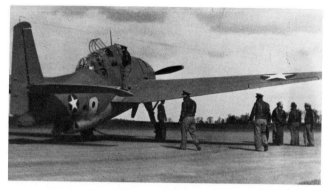

Above: In 1942, a year after the Eastern Aircraft Division plant was opened, the first Grumman Avenger naval torpedo plane was tested at Trenton. The plane was approved, and the assembly line was soon producing eight planes a day. Courtesy, Trentoniana Collection, TFPL

Below: Workers at the Philco electric plant pose with servicemen in this World War II scene. Thousands were employed in skilled precision work in Trenton's industries during the war. Courtesy, Trentoniana Collection, TFPL

Above: The original New Jersey State Capitol was designed by Jonathan Doane of Trenton and built in 1792. This lithograph (c. 1845) was made by Thomas Sinclair from an earlier drawing by A. Frey and shows the original State House that still stands as a section of the present Capitol building. (NJHS)

Below: Only the bell tower of the First United Methodist Church looks today as it did in this 1870s postcard. Looking up South Broad to State, the Philadelphia Bargain Store is visible; across the street is A.V. Manning's furniture store, the owner's initials appearing above the roofline of neighboring buildings. The awnings date the picture, since the Common Council banned them from downtown businesses in 1902. Courtesy, Trentoniana Collection, TFPL

Facing page top: When George Washington passed through Trenton on his way to the first presidential inauguration in 1789, he was given a reception by the ladies of the town. A century later this scene was painted by J. Califano showing the triumphal arch of 13 wooden spans that was erected on the Assunpink Creek bridge. Courtesy, Collection of Mr. and Mrs. John A. Harney of Trenton

Facing page bottom: In his oil painting "Trenton Barracks with Parade of Redcoats," local artist William E. Pedrick recreated an 18th-century scene. As a few civilians watch, the British garrison marches through a gate in the wooden palisade. The first British troops to occupy the Barracks in 1758 were part of the Inniskilling Regiment of Foot. Courtesy, The Old Barracks Museum

Previous page: The Dutch and the Swedes began to map the area that was to become New Jersey before the arrival of the English settlers. This early map of "New Belgium, New England, and Virchinia" by N. Visscher shows the Delaware Valley and its tributaries that influenced the early development of Trenton. The illustrations also show a Seneca Indian village, a Dutch town with its typical windmill, and the ships of the period. (NJSL)

Left: The idea was E.C. Hill's; the design was Frederick Law Olmsted's. Thanks to the persistence of Hill, the country's foremost landscape architect was hired to give Trenton a park in 1888. The city paid a little less than $700 an acre for the 100 acres it bought. Although Cadwalader (note the misspelling on the postcard) did not open officially until 1902, people flocked to it from the 1890s on. The park's popularity stimulated the city's westward expansion. Courtesy, Trentoniana Collection, TFPL

Below: The first steamer Burlington appeared on the Delaware River in 1827, and there was still a ship of the same name in operation on the Philadelphia-Trenton run in 1910. Courtesy, Trentoniana Collection, TFPL

Above: The historic Mill Hill section is the oldest part of the city. Here Victorian houses replaced the earlier colonial structures. In time these fell into neglect, but for the past 20 years residents have been restoring the beauty of the Victorian architecture as seen in this view of Mr. Robert Allen's house on Jackson Street. Photograph by Don Reichman

Left: Mid-18th-century Philadelphia Chippendale-style chairs surround a Queen Anne dining table set with Chinese export porcelain in the well-known "Canton" and "Fitzhugh" patterns. Courtesy, The Colonial Dames of America Collection, Old Barracks Museum, photograph by Barry Coleman

Facing page bottom: The yellow Raceabout (shown here) was the most popular model produced by the Mercer Automobile Company. The Roebling and Kuser families operated the company from 1910 to 1919 on Whitehead Road. Neither cheap nor abundant, this Raceabout (now owned by Henry Austin Clark) sold for $2,500 and was capable of speeds of 70 miles per hour when most cars' top speed was 40. Courtesy, Automobile Quarterly Magazine

Above: The Scottish merchant, William Trent, having made a fortune in Philadelphia, eventually moved to the Falls of the Delaware where he purchased 800 acres from the Quaker, Mahlon Stacy, Jr. In 1719 the Trent House, a gem of colonial-style architecture, was built. In 1929 its owner, Edward Stokes, donated the building to the City of Trenton, and the house has since been restored and furnished in the 18th-century style. Courtesy, The Trent House, photograph by Barry Coleman

Right: The beautifully restored parlor of the Trent House conveys an atmosphere of colonial elegance. In this view high-backed carved William and Mary chairs stand beside an ornate card table. The 18th-century corner cupboard is decorated with an inlaid oriental pattern. Each year many children from the Trenton schools see a glimpse of the past while being shown through the house. Courtesy, The Trent House, photograph by Barry Coleman

Left: Robert L. Hooper, the owner of the Trent House in 1767, advertised the property for sale in the Pennsylvania Journal as "a genteel brick dwelling house, 40 x 48 feet, two stories high, four rooms on a floor, with a large, handsome staircase and entry, with a cellar under the whole building, and a courtyard on each front of the house." The carved wooden staircase is still in its original location in the main hall. Courtesy, The Trent House, photograph by Barry Coleman

Below: The English William and Mary style furniture of the Trent House dining room established a tone of dignified elegance. On a polished circular table pewter dishes gleam under the Flemish brass chandelier. The fireplace is decorated with 18th-century paneling, and the original flooring has been preserved. Courtesy, The Trent House, photograph by Barry Coleman

Above: The "Trenton Vase," porcelain, 1904, The Trenton Potteries Company (1892-1967), height 54 inches. One of four monumental works made for the Trenton Potteries display at the Louisiana Purchase Exposition in St. Louis, the vase depicts Emanuel Leutze's famous painting of "Washington Crossing the Delaware, 1776" on one side. The vase was produced at the Empire Pottery, located at North Clinton Avenue at Ott Street, one of five firms that merged in 1892 to form the Trenton Potteries Company. Gift of the Trenton Potteries Company, NJSM

Top: Plate, porcelain, ca. 1910, decorated by Hans Nosek for Lenox, Inc., (1906-present), diameter 10 inches. Delicate hand painting and elaborate raised gold work are the hallmarks of the best decorations created at Lenox. Courtesy, Lenox, Inc.

Above: Presidential dinnerware, porcelain, 1918-1951, Lenox, Inc., (1906-present), diameter 10½ inches. Lenox's distinctive belleek dinnerware was chosen by President Woodrow Wilson to replace the White House Wedgwood service. Presidents Warren G. Harding, Calvin Coolidge, and Herbert Hoover continued to use the patterns for the service plate (left) and dinner plate (center) chosen by President Wilson, while President Franklin D. Roosevelt ordered a new design (right) during his administration. Courtesy, Lenox, Inc.

Above: The True American was a prominent 19th-century local newspaper that was bought by the Trenton Times in 1913. In this watercolor painting by local artist Marge Chavooshian, the newspaper building, which was erected in 1893, appears between two older houses. To the left, on the corner of Hanover and North Warren streets, the hotel that Abraham Lincoln visited in 1861 is still standing. Courtesy, Marge Chavooshian

Bottom right: The building on the corner of South Broad and Market streets, once a drugstore, has since become the popular Joe's Mill Hill Saloon, featuring Victorian decor. Artist Tom Malloy recalls when these shops were part of a large Orthodox Jewish community where, in pre-Depression days, Trentonians came to buy live fish and fresh bakery treats from the kosher stores. Courtesy, Thomas Malloy

Right: In the silent movie era, the Princess Theatre was the most popular entertainment palace in east Trenton. The children's matinee and the Saturday night shows were crowded with devoted fans through the 1920s and into the Depression years. One rainy morning local artist Tom Malloy painted the theater, which stood on the corner of North Clinton Avenue and Meade Street, recapturing the nostalgia of its vanished past. Courtesy, Thomas Malloy

Above: The Trenton Railroad Station is a familiar scene to those who commute to work in New York and Philadelphia. Long-distance passenger trains, locals, and heavy freights rumble through the station at frequent intervals. Business people, shoppers, and students mingle while waiting on the platform for the next train in this painting by local artist Mel Leipzig. Courtesy, Mel Leipzig

Right: "Cedric Jensen and His Jazz Group at the Original Trenton Coffee House" is the title of this painting by Mel Leipzig. In the evening Trentonians gather in the center city area, near the shopping mall, to hear a wide range of music. Courtesy, Mel Leipzig

Facing page: "I observed from an art point of view that Trenton was changing, that old Trenton was disappearing, and so I decided to do something to preserve some of its memories." With these words artist Tom Malloy explained his philosophical perspective. His series of watercolor paintings faithfully records the passing scene. In this view the Battle Monument stands as a symbol of Trenton's past. Courtesy, Thomas Malloy

Above left: A summer Saturday in Cadwalader Park would not be complete without the presence of the balloon man. A generation of Trenton's children have seen his familiar figure at the entrance to the park. Photograph by Don Reichman

Left: Trenton's spacious Cadwalader Park was designed in the 19th-century romantic style by the noted architect Frederick Law Olmsted. For the delight of children a small deer park is maintained in a rustic setting. Photograph by Don Reichman

Above: Trenton's Heritage Days Festival is held annually in June in Mill Hill Park. Close by is the site of Mahlon Stacy's Mill on Assunpink Creek. This fair owes its popularity to its ethnic and cultural flavor and diversity. Costumes, crafts, and special foods are displayed in an atmosphere of fun and friendship. Photograph by Don Reichman

Facing page bottom: On a hot summer day nothing attracts children like running water. These children play in a cooling spray in the Mill Hill section. Photograph by Nan Wright

Above: During the 1960s the State of
New Jersey gave visible proof of its faith
in the city's future by engaging in a
major building program. The modern
Labor and Industry Building dates from
this period. Photograph by Don
Reichman

Right: Artist Mel Leipzig caught the
spirit of the downtown Trenton scene in
this painting of Willow Street. To the
left is the tall Kelsey Building of Edison
College and the gray stone Old

Barracks, while to the right is the white
office building of the State Treasury and
the old and new Masonic halls.
Pedestrians pass along a street lined on
both sides by 18th- and 20th-century
buildings. Courtesy, Mel Leipzig

Facing page: Viewed across the
Delaware River at twilight, Trenton's
central cultural area is surmounted by
the illuminated golden dome of the state
capitol. Courtesy, State of New Jersey

Chapter Eight

TOWARD A RENAISSANCE

"Lorenzo's" restaurant is a familiar gathering place for Trentonians who savor its delicacies while relaxing in rooms filled with ornate Victorian decor. In this painting by Mel Leipzig, Mike, the bartender, presides over the conversation of politicians, residents, and students. "Lorenzo's" symbolizes Trenton's appreciation for its past and its future. Courtesy, Mel Leipzig

The forties found the city's downtown streets filled with khaki or navy-blue clad men and women of the armed forces. Throughout the war years the numbers of local servicemen were greatly increased by busloads of soldiers from nearby military establishments, especially from the Burlington County acreage named Fort Dix.

Trentonians were already familiar with the Army's Fort Dix, since it was their own Company C of the National Guard that had been dispatched there in June 1917 to begin laying out what was then Camp Dix. The recruits had been assembled by the Trenton Engineers Club and they transformed the farms and woodland near Wrightstown into a very large military post. Appropriately enough, the same Company C, after serving in France—having sailed from and returned to the Hoboken docks—was demobilized at Camp Dix in late May 1919.

By the early 1940s improved transportation made it much easier for soldiers with night passes to come to Trenton. One of the first USOs in the country was established by a consortium of local service organizations which opened a center on Warren Street, less than two blocks from the bus terminal, on June 22, 1942. Shortly after the first was opened, a second club opened at the YMCA near the train station. A third USO was operated during the war by the YM-YWHA at their building at 18 South Stockton Street. Before the last USO was closed on April 28, 1947, servicemen and women clocked 1,250,000 visits to one of the Trenton clubs.

The USO was revived for the Korean War on July 1, 1952 when the former Hibernian Club at 132 North Warren Street was acquired. The USO Club continued to welcome military personnel into the 1970s, supported by an annual budget appropriation from the Delaware Valley United Way.

Local folklore offers a story indicative of the impact made by the proximity of so many soldiers at Fort Dix on the comfortable small-town atmosphere of Trenton. Local public officials were concerned that the influx of soldiers coming into the city looking for a few hours of relaxation would attract large numbers of prostitutes. Thinking of their wives, daughters, sisters, and mothers going downtown for shopping and cultural events, the story tells of the officials' creative solution to keep residents safely walking the streets. According to the story, a secret meeting between powerful gangland leaders and city officials resulted in a working arrangement whereby gambling activities were overlooked in exchange for restricting prostitution to a few downtown blocks, to operate primarily out of houses. While prostitution was restricted, many other businesses thrived, including center city restaurants which were open 24 hours a day to serve the military and the greatly swollen civilian work force.

The state government, under the leadership of Governor Charles Edison (the inventor's son) braved the rationing and shortages of the wartime economy while looking to the future. Despite the need for a new state constitution to revamp the antiquated systems prescribed by the 1844 New Jersey constitution, the citizens voted their preference to wait until the war was over and the men were back home to adopt a new framework of government. Finally in 1947 a modern constitution was ratified, inaugurating an era of greatly expanding government services soon apparent in new buildings to house the clearly defined executive department, the efficient judicial branch, and the stronger legislative branch.

While State Archivist and Trenton native Sidney Goldmann gathered the official records to document the great changes the government was undergoing, other officials were considering more radical changes in Trenton's skyline. The golden dome of the State House, added in 1847 to the original 1790 building, had proclaimed the city as the state capital. Because of the building's poor maintenance for over a decade, plans were proposed to raze the State House, with the exception of the dome section (rebuilt in 1889), and to construct new, modern high-rise office buildings. But because of the unemployment and the housing shortage facing returning military personnel, the state legislature responded to citizen pressure by diverting funds appropriated for the proposed 13-story government office building to a project for new housing for veterans. Under subsequent governors, persuasive representatives from the city were able to win support for refurbishing the pre-1940 state structures. More importantly, the planned dispersal of the state's functions out of Trenton was halted after the completion of one building in suburban Ewing Township. The Highway Department moved out of the city to Parkway Avenue in the summer of 1950. Already Governor Walter E. Edge preferred Princeton's historic Morven as the executive mansion, and left it to the state of New Jersey for just such a use. From 1957 to 1981, four governors occupied the mansion as their official and their personal home. A larger, though not as historic, house named Drumthwacket—also in Prince-

ton—was restored and modernized by private contributors as a more comfortable and gracious residence for any future governor who chooses to live there.

Major construction projects were inaugurated in downtown Trenton in the vicinity of the State House once the state government overcame the general tendency to fly to suburbia and committed itself to being a part of a renewed urban area. Between 1959 and 1965, eight substantial buildings were constructed by the state government in concert with the city's first urban renewal efforts.

City officials were not blind to the traffic congestion and to the deteriorating physical appearance of large portions of Trenton. It was, they thought, the reason why the Mercer County suburbs grew 40.1 percent between 1940 and 1950 while the city registered only a 2.7 percent increase. The Greater Trenton Chamber of Commerce hired a professional researcher in 1957 who showed demographically the correlation between the areas of heavy population and blight—principally those that encircled the center city business core—and the frequency of juvenile crime.

Above: Servicemen from nearby Camp Dix frequented the Trenton USO. Here local hostesses enliven a dance in the ballroom of the New Masonic Temple during World War II. Courtesy, Trentoniana Collection, TFPL

Facing page: In December 1960, a blizzard gripped Trenton. Traffic halted, and pedestrians walked to work on East State Street. Yard's department store then occupied the old city hall on the corner to the left. The traditional holiday decorations add a festive touch to the scene. Courtesy, The Trenton Times

An analysis of the city's tax base revealed that three levels of government occupied valuable commercial land while adding nothing to the city's tax coffers. Yet these government facilities placed more and more demands on traffic control, fire protection, street cleaning, and other city services. The majority of property bought for non-residential use in the 1950s and 1960s was by tax-exempt organizations. Trenton thus faced sharply declining tax revenues at a time when much of the population was becoming dependent on governmental welfare programs.

A solution discussed openly since the 1930s was regional consolidation based on Trenton's annexing the

adjoining townships of Ewing, Hamilton, and Lawrence. The city's higher tax rate was the reason given for rejection of the proposal by township residents. City voters in turn thought that extending their municipal services would increase their already costly tax burden. Annexation remains an unlikely solution to the city's problems.

Into the 1950s Trenton had been such a comfortable town that its numerous boosters confidently wrote of its "uniquely bright potential as the trading, cultural and social center . . . of the region." That, they believed, was to be achieved by professionally planned future development based on federal programs for urban renewal. The city government undertook the task with an impressive agenda. A stricter housing code was adopted in 1952 and 1956, a new filtration plant was constructed for the water works, streets were repaved, and traffic flow was eased by the completion of the John Fitch Way. The penalty for this improvement, however, was the dissection of the riverfront Stacy Park.

Some of the impetus for this activity arose out of the unwelcomed spotlight that Trenton found itself in as it garnered international publicity as the subject of the study known as "Case City"—a research project on a "typical" blighted medium-sized American town. That town was Trenton, and the results of the study made by 45 graduate students in urban planning at the University of Pennsylvania were written up in *House and Home* magazine in October 1957 under the headline "Nightmare or Dream?" The scathing article announced that 80 percent of the housing supply in Trenton was over 50 years old, and that once-elegant neighborhoods were no longer desirable since "most of the nice people live out of the city." The 25 percent jump in the black population (14,450 in 1950 to 18,000 in 1956) was described, in bold type, as a serious problem in a city whose total population had remained static. The article further stated that suburbs in the same six-year period rose from 320,000 to 420,000 residents, and that the flight to the suburbs would be in full force by 1980. The warnings were heeded, and an ambitious, long-term program was undertaken to wipe out the blight threatening to destroy not only Trenton but the small-town way of life it represented. Ironically, the success or failure of these efforts would depend on whether or not local neighborhoods could be retained and Trenton's small-town ambience reinforced.

Trenton's urban renewal program began in the postwar period with the building of low-income housing projects. In the era when segregation still prevailed, the Donnelly Homes were designed for white residents and the Lincoln Homes along the canal in north Trenton were planned for black residents. The first large-scale project was the renewal of the old Coalport district. In the 19th century it had been the bustling center of the pottery companies where coal and china clay were unloaded from barges on the Delaware and Raritan Canal. After the closing of the canal the area became derelict. An extensive tract of land was cleared and in the 1960s industries were offered inducements to relocate there. The enterprises which presently occupy the area along Perry Street include *The Trenton Times, The Trentonian,* and the Trenton Police Headquarters. Still vacant acres testify to the failure of the Coalport renewal to attract new industries, new jobs, and taxpaying manufacturing plants.

By 1958 city officials were cooperating with the New Jersey state authorities in implementing the John Fitch Way Urban Renewal project. Named in honor of the inventor of the steamboat, the John Fitch Way was built beside the Delaware River, through Stacy Park, to provide rapid access between the city center and the suburbs. A large area from the river's edge to Broad Street and from Assunpink Creek to the lower bridge was cleared. The houses that were removed, although decayed, were some of the oldest in the city in a neighborhood that held nostalgic memories for many Trentonians of immigrant ancestry. These houses were replaced by buildings for the State Labor and Industry Department, the Agriculture and Health Departments, and by the Justice Complex, the latter just completed in 1982. During the same period the Kingsbury Towers housing units were built on Market Street to attract middle-income state workers to reside in the city. The complex consisted of two high-rise towers and several two-story houses and apartments. The apartments have become occupied by low-income families in the 1980s and the towers are being converted to senior citizen housing. The Miller Homes were built in the 1960s on the edge of Coalport at Seward and Lincoln streets as a low-income relocation project for those who were forced to move by the John Fitch Way scheme.

As early as the 1950s a few families began to see the bargains and possibilities in buying homes in a 19th century neighborhood at a bend in the Assunpink Creek, called Mill Hill, where houses were decayed but structurally sound. Mayor Arthur Holland earned national publicity when he moved to this integrated area in 1964. These few blocks were then adopted by the city as the Mercer-Jackson project and became a model for the revitalization of old residential neighborhoods. City planners pursued a policy of acquisition, selective demolition, and rehabilitation. A three-percent mortgage rate was offered to residents who would restore existing structures, and a few new dwellings were erected.

The rehabilitation policy was extended in the 1970s into an area named Center City South. After the removal of a defunct department store, Mill Hill Park was established beside Assunpink Creek where the Second Battle of Trenton was fought in 1777. A statue of Washington and the Douglass House were placed on the edge of the park near an old stone church which became the Mill Hill Playhouse. Within sight of the park the red brick high-rise for senior citizens known as Architect's Housing was built. In front of the long brick row of stores on South Broad Street, from Market Street to Centre Street, the city planted trees, laid brick sidewalks, and improved street lighting to preserve the old commercial district.

When Carmen Armenti was mayor in the late 1960s, the former New Jersey Armory, built in 1905, was purchased by the city for use as a civic center. Large

Above: The New Jersey State Armory was completed in 1905 and was a Trenton landmark for over 60 years. In the late 1960s, when Carmen J. Armenti was mayor, the city used the building as a civic center. Governor William Cahill's inaugural ball was held here and the large auditorium was used for basketball, boxing, wrestling, the Shriner circus, and concerts. When it burned down in 1975 many city records were lost. Courtesy, Trentoniana Collection, TFPL

Facing page: The John Fitchway urban renewal project has produced changes in Trenton's skyline. In the center are the Kingsbury Towers built for middle- and low-income families in the late 1950s. On the left stands the Luther Arms

senior citizen apartment building which opened in the 1970s, while on the right is the New Jersey State Justice Complex, completed in 1982. Funding came from private, municipal, state, and federal financing.

Below: One of the major civic improvements in the downtown area was the completion of the new wing of the Trenton Free Public Library in 1976 under the leadership of City Librarian Veronica Cary. The older portion of the library was built in 1902 on the site of the Trenton Academy. Above the level of the Ionic columns are carved the names of famous literary figures.

While Mayor Arthur Holland was in office, the site was soon cleared for the construction of a new annex to the Municipal Building which was ready for occupancy in 1978. Another physical improvement in the downtown area was the completion of the new wing of the Trenton Free Public Library in 1976 under the leadership of the City Librarian, Veronica Cary. Both of these new structures are prime examples of the steady revival of Trenton's urban core by governmental agencies.

In keeping with the city planning concepts of the 1970s, the Trenton Commons was formed by closing State Street to traffic for two blocks between Montgomery and Warren streets. Trees, brick paving, and modern street lights were provided to enhance the appearance of the downtown shopping mall.

The neglected North Ward was the scene of an ambitious new housing program which began in 1977. Named for a local voting district, the North 25 housing development was constructed on a 16-acre lot which was once the Reading Railroad yard. Funding was obtained from the New Jersey Housing Finance Agency, but unlike other projects, the planning was done in consultation with civic leaders and local residents. The development was built in response to the need for public housing above the poverty level and to improve the depressed area under the shadow of the Battle Monument. The several buildings of the project are north of the canal from Warren Street to Calhoun Street. The 11-story Bernice J. Munce Tower, named in honor of a respected public school teacher, is designed for senior citizens while the red brick two-story apartment units are for other families. The Austin Health Center offers clinical services which are free for those who are receiving welfare payments. Well-designed structures with

audiences attended events such as basketball, boxing, wrestling, the Shriner circus, and concerts. Governor William Cahill's inaugural ball as well as political rallies were held in the auditorium. In 1975 the Armory burned down and many valuable city records were lost.

109

adequate lighting and proper maintenance are this attractive community's assets.

Trenton's churches still play their traditional role as neighborhood centers of education, civic improvement, and social concern. Catholic charities, the Presbyterian day nursery, the Salvation Army, and the Baptist social agencies are examples. When federal funding became available for senior citizen housing, the Brothers of Israel built two high-rise apartments on Greenwood Avenue named Trent Center East and West. A Lutheran project, Luther Towers, was built on West State Street. In the center city rehabilitation area on South Broad Street, the Luther Arms apartments were erected as a facility for the elderly and handicapped. Commercial companies built several luxury high-rise structures including the Capital Plaza Inn, the Carteret Arms, and the Lafayette House on West State Street.

By the 1980s Trenton's city planners had accepted the concept of repair and adaptive usage of old buildings which were still structurally sound. A huge area of derelict factories was available in east and south Trenton following the closing of the potteries and steel mills. The abandoned Stokely-Van Camp vegetable canning factory on Lalor Street was converted into a publicly subsidized housing development called South Village. The attractive project which opened in 1982 contains 344 apartments for senior citizens.

To aid in saving Trenton's heritage, seven historic districts have been defined. These are Berkeley Square, Mill Hill, State House, South Warren Street, Greenwood/Hamilton, Hanover/Academy, and Yard Avenue. The pride of Trentonians in their neighborhoods has been encouraged by city officials as one of the strongest factors in the life of the community. Neighborhoods such as Glen Afton, Hiltonia, and Cadwalader Heights are restoring buildings and improving civic services for their residents. Old streets such as Centre or Hamilton are lined with a fascinating variety of frame or brick houses built in every style of the past two centuries, and taxpayers have again discovered the charms of living within the city.

Recent efforts have been aimed at strengthening ethnic neighborhoods. Rehabilitation of older houses, if not actual restoration, generally succeeds. The ethnic areas of today are attractive combinations of specialty stores, bakeshops, churches, and parochial schools where residents feel comfortable walking the streets. Here congregate the largest ethnic groups: Italian, Polish, Ger-

man, Ukrainian, and Hungarian. In addition to English, the spoken languages are Spanish, Italian, Polish, and Yiddish.

To celebrate the city's ethnic heritage the Commons Commission, in 1979, organized the remarkably popular Heritage Days Festival. On a weekend in early June over 100,000 people gather to shop, talk, watch entertainment, and eat at the more than two dozen ethnic food stands in Mill Hill Park and on the downtown Commons. The crafts, music, and dancing under the colorful tents, and the appeal to all groups, who join in a friendly atmosphere, ensure its popularity.

A recent, popular Trenton attraction is the State Street Stroll, begun in 1978, with the focus on the State House Historic District. Each year the street in front of the Capitol is closed to automobiles on the first Sunday after Labor Day. The emphasis is on historic preservation and old-fashioned displays and activities such as the annual croquet game, antique cars, high-wheel bicycles, and a tour of historic homes, all at the instigation of civic activist Rosalie Dietz.

Families still line the curbsides for Trenton's Thanksgiving Parade, the last of the numerous annual parades that were held in the city years ago. Established ethnic groups, such as the Italians, with their Columbus Day Parade in October, and new ones such as the Puerto Ricans with their Sunday Puerto Rican Parade in August, add colorful public activities to the community calendar. In mid-September the Italian community celebrates the Feast of Maria Santissima di Casadrino, popularly known as the Feast of Lights. Religious devo-

Facing page: The first synagogue was established in Trenton in 1860. This picture shows the Har Sinai Temple on Bellevue Avenue which opened in 1929.

Below: Hundreds of performers and thousands of spectators gathered for the annual Sports Night in 1957 in the Trenton High School gym. After months of rehearsing, the enthusiastic students presented a colorful show of dancing, music, and drama. Those evening entertainments are still recalled with nostalgic fondness by many Trentonians. Courtesy, The Trenton Times

Right: The venerable Kelsey Building on West State Street has played a vital educational role in Trenton for over 70 years. Built in 1911 for the School of Industrial Arts, the building contained Trenton Junior College from 1947 to 1967. For a few years Mercer County Community College used the classrooms. The Kelsey Building is now the main location of Edison State College.

tion combines with neighborhood spirit as friendly blocks are decorated with strings of lights, a tradition since the early years of this century.

An award designating Trenton "All-America City" was presented by the National Municipal League in 1966. The *Look* magazine article announcing the award

mentioned in particular the Theatre-in-the-Park summer project in addition to the construction of the new state buildings as visible evidence of local citizens' commitment to revitalization of the city, especially in the eight years since the "Case City" expose.

Despite the city's many improvements, the impressive physical changes made by the city government were not the hoped-for panacea: a frightening point made vividly clear to planners and politicians by the riots and demonstrations that burst upon the city streets following the assassination of Martin Luther King, Jr. on April 4, 1968. Reporting on the first of several disturbances that racked up property damage, personal injuries, and a long-term legacy of fear of the city streets, the local news headlines calmly wrote, "Negro Teen Gangs Disrupt Trenton." Thirteen years later the mayor told a *New York Times* reporter that "the city schools and the fear of crime were keeping people away" from Trenton. The population of 92,124 was 47 percent black, 8 percent Hispanic, and 45 percent white, according to the 1980 census, and there had been a total population loss of 12 percent since 1970. By the 1970s Trenton had also lost half its manufacturing jobs while the number of manufacturing businesses dropped by a third, leaving government as the city's most reliable employer.

In a descriptive analysis of Trenton by reporter Daniel Akst in 1981, the small-town atmosphere that pervades the community is listed as a distinctive, positive feature for the area. So are the two daily newspapers (the only city in New Jersey to have such), the Mercer Metro bus system, the railroad connections with other Jersey towns, the large employment centers of Philadelphia and New York, the 20-minute drive from State House to farmland, and, of course, the city's vital neighborhoods.

In 1973 the Trenton Historical Society began to restore the Old Eagle Tavern, which is one of the city's

Above: For two centuries the citizens of Trenton have lined the streets to cheer Presidents as they pass by. George Washington, John Adams, Abraham Lincoln, Woodrow Wilson, and Calvin Coolidge made memorable visits. In 1951, 10,000 people watched Dwight D. Eisenhower as he drove along State Street on the way to the War Memorial building. Courtesy, The Trenton Times

Facing page top: As part of the renewal of the inner city, the historic Eagle Tavern was restored through the cooperative efforts of the Trenton Historical Society and local unions with city, county, state, and federal support. Work began in 1973 on the building which had been a Quaker residence in

the 18th century and a popular tavern in the 19th century. In 1980 the Eagle Tavern reopened as an attractive restaurant to serve the center city area.

Facing page bottom: The Trenton Marine Terminal is equipped with gantry and caterpillar cranes and 19 cargo masts to handle three freighters at once at peak capacity. The imports include rubber, clay, iron, lumber, feldspar, and cork. Trenton's factories export tile, steel wire, tires, textiles, and electrical appliances. Here the Essex Druid of England and the Heroy of Norway are unloading china clay. Courtesy, The Trenton Times

few remaining pre-Revolutionary War buildings. It was built at South Broad and Ferry streets between 1765 and 1772 by the Quaker, Jesse Waln, who was the manager of the gristmill on Assunpink Creek. The four-story brick residence was one of the largest buildings in Trenton during the Revolutionary War and at that time occupied a commanding position on the main road to the lower ferry across the Delaware River. The Tavern, which is listed in the National Register of Historic Places, was reopened as a restaurant on Christmas Day 1980 and has become part of the revival of the center city area.

The historic Douglass House, where Washington held a council of his officers in 1777, was acquired by the city and moved to Mill Hill Park. In the midst of beautiful Cadwalader Park stands Ellarslie, a Victorian mansion built for Henry McCall by the architect John Notman in 1846. With the aid of federal funds, the Italianate resi-

dence was restored and reopened in 1977 as the City Museum. The Adams and Sickles pharmacy building on the corner of West State and Prospect streets was restored by the city and later sold to a private group. Next door the old Canal House, built between 1850 and 1870, was also restored by the city to accommodate a tenant. In addition, the Delaware and Raritan Canal bridge tender's small wooden house was placed on the state and national registers of historic landmarks.

Some of the city's historic houses are privately owned. "The Hermitage" on Colonial Avenue, once the home of Revolutionary War General Philemon Dickinson, has become an apartment house. Bow Hill, the handsome brick mansion near the river in South Trenton, built by Barnt DeKlyn in 1787 and tenanted by Joseph Bonaparte in 1820, is being cared for by a Ukrainian church group.

Beyond the city limits, the township historical societies have carried on the work of historic preservation. The carefully restored 18th century Abbott farmhouse is now the headquarters of the Hamilton Township Historical Society. In 1976 the Township of Hamilton purchased the 22-acre Kuser Farm with the assistance of New Jersey Green Acres Funds. Within three years the Kuser Farm Park and 1892 mansion were opened to the public.

The oldest house in the region is also located in Hamilton Township. In 1708 the Quaker settler Isaac Watson built a stone house on his 800-acre estate near the river, and in 1964 it was adopted as a preservation project by the Daughters of the American Revolution and by Mercer County.

In Ewing Township near Federal City Road stands the Benjamin Temple house, a typical colonial farmhouse built between 1710 and 1750. Also in Ewing Township plans are being presented for the restoration of the Green farmhouse, built in 1717, which stands on the Trenton State College campus.

Rider College in Lawrence Township has preserved the pre-Revolutionary War Benjamin Van Cleve house, which now serves as an admissions office at the front entrance to the campus. The determined efforts of the Lawrence Township Historical Society have resulted in the restoration of the 19th-century Port Mercer canal house. A museum is planned for the little wooden building alongside the Delaware and Raritan Canal which is now the society's headquarters.

A private group has been formed to preserve the John

Rogers farmhouse in Mercer County Park, which is the only remaining Revolutionary War-era house in West Windsor Township.

As a result of these preservation efforts the Trenton vicinity has developed its visible history into a rich resource, one that illustrates the American 18th and 19th-century heritage.

Since the colonial era Trenton's residents have enjoyed various sports. Washington and his friends fished for perch and shad in the swift-flowing Delaware, and frozen creeks and ponds have provided winter ice skating for three centuries. During the 19th century Trenton's Eagle Racecourse was a center for thoroughbred racing which was replaced in the 20th century by auto racing at the State Fairgrounds.

English potters brought with them their native skills in soccer and soon established teams and leagues. Newspapers in those days reported English soccer teams' scores because of keen local interest. The sons of the potters went on to play on industrial, high school, and college teams. Olympic Soccer team members included the younger Al Cooper in 1928, George "Shorty" Nemchick, who later worked for the city, and Pete Pietras, who became a fireman. National soccer championships were won by the Trenton Junior College team in 1963 and by Mercer County Community College Teams in 1968 and 1982.

The first professional basketball game in the nation was played in Trenton in 1896 in association with the old YMCA in the second Masonic Temple at State and Broad streets. Captain Fred Cooper, his brother Al, Harry Huff, Albert Bratton, and Charley Kline were pioneers of basketball. They developed the short pass and other early innovations. Fred Cooper designed the modern uniform and became the first coach of Princeton's basketball team. In the era of the 1920s the Trenton Tigers were a powerful team and one of their players, Tom Barlow, is now a member of the Basketball Hall of Fame. At Trenton High School Coach Leroy "Red" Smith produced some of the best school teams in the country from 1920 to 1960, and Mercer County Community College teams won two national basketball championships in 1973 and 1974.

In baseball Trenton has played host to several renowned teams. During the earliest days of the sport, the tough Trenton Atlantics competed against the Philadelphia Athletics and much later the Trenton Giants played before enthusiastic crowds of 10,000 fans at

Dunn Field from 1946 to 1950. Willie Mays, who later rose to fame as a major league player, was an outfielder for the Trenton Giants. Another baseball player from Trenton was George Washington Case, Jr. For 11 years in the American League, all but one with the Washington Senators, he was "the fastest man in baseball," able to circle the bases in 13.7 seconds. In 1939 and 1946 he led the majors in stolen bases and his career total was 349. He later became a coach, scout, and field office representative. On October 11, 1927, factories and schools closed and 3,500 people assembled to see Babe Ruth playing first base and Lou Gehrig playing the outfield with the City League All Stars against the black Brooklyn Royal Giants. Ruth hit three home runs on the old Trenton high school field and one ball landed over the centerfield fence near the drugstore at Chambers and Liberty streets.

In 1945 Trenton's best-known boxer, Ike Williams, became the National Boxing Association lightweight champion and defended his title as world lightweight champion from 1947 to 1951. Sammy Goss was a member of the U.S. Olympic team in Mexico City in 1968 and was later the North American junior lightweight champion.

The coach who trained many local swimming champions was Al Neuschaefer. From 1932 until he retired in 1960, he made the Tornadoes of Trenton High School a nationally known team. In those 29 years Trenton won 19 New Jersey state championships and seven national interscholastic championships, and set many national and world records.

Although he later became a pro football player, Elvin

Facing page: Before he rose to fame in the major leagues, Willie Mays was a popular local player with the Trenton Giants. He was a swift outfielder at the old Dunn Field before crowds of 10,000 loyal Trentonians who watched the Giants play between 1946 and 1950. Courtesy, The Trenton Times

Above: In 11 years in the American League, all but one with the Washington Senators, Trentonian George Washington Case, Jr., was considered

"the fastest man in baseball." He could circle the bases in 13.7 seconds. Case led the majors in stolen bases in 1939 and 1946. Courtesy, The Trenton Times

Above right: Ike Williams began his career as a local Trenton boxer and turned pro in 1940. He became the National Boxing Association lightweight champion in 1945 and was the world lightweight champion between 1947 and 1951. Courtesy, The Trenton Times

Bethea of the Houston Oilers set double national records in shot put and discus in 1964 as a member of the Trenton High School track team. He went on to a 15-year football career and was seven times a Pro Bowl player.

Another sport brought by the English potters was quoits, which soon had hundreds of teams and thousands of players. It remained popular through the Prohibition era when every speakeasy had a quoit court behind the premises. The English also brought lawn bowling, and two greens are still used in Cadwalader Park. The rich heritage of local sports continues at present in the popularity of golf, tennis, bocce, jogging, and bicycling, activities supported by local parks, especially by the Mercer County Park Commission.

Contributing a new force in the cultural life of the capital area is the Trenton Artists Workshop Association (TAWA), organized by Mary T. Howard and Lotta Patterson in 1978. They helped change Trenton's negative cultural image with "Eyes on Trenton," a 7-week festival of art, poetry, music, and theater held in 1981.

The festival involved the city's major cultural institutions such as the State Museum, Ellarslie (the City Museum), and the War Memorial, as well as the Mill Hill Playhouse, the Original Trenton Coffeehouse, and the Performing Arts Committee of Trinity Episcopal Cathedral. TAWA not only flourished, it supported the development of related groups such as T'MPO, the Trenton Music Performance Organization. TAWA has come a long way in educating the public about the tremendous amount of talent in the area by exhibiting the work of local artists at public sites. These artists are enthusiastic supporters of Trenton's cultural renaissance.

From the time, unrecorded but known, when the Indians established campsites on the river bluffs, individuals and groups have come to the falls of the Delaware and decided it was a good place to live. So many came that it developed into a metropolitan area, providing a way of life and a quality of life, that was personal, productive, varied, and invigorating on a human scale. It is today a multicultural and interdependent community of town, suburb, and rapidly disappearing rural area. It is still pervaded by the small-town spirit of family commitment and individual friendship. It is this spirit of commitment and friendship that gets things accomplished. The townships in Mercer County cannot really plan on a thriving populous region, swelling around a center that is bankrupt. Trenton is the state capital and its rejuvenation will make an urban community that is aptly described as a capital place. There are those who, in their lives, their work, and their public service, want to carry on the heritage of earlier residents who took pride in their association with Trenton.

115

Chapter Nine

PARTNERS IN PROGRESS

by Sally Lane

Trenton's commercial roots extend all the way back to its settlement in 1679 by an Englishman with an eye for business prospects: Mahlon Stacy built his gristmill on the Assunpink Creek after determining that the inhabitants of West Jersey had no other mill.

The town's 18th-century growth depended to a large extent on its location as the farthest point that travelers could reach by land on their journey from New York to Philadelphia. That location, and the importance for shipping of both the Delaware River and the Delaware & Raritan Canal, were the first factors ironmaker Peter Cooper mentioned to John A. Roebling when urging him to locate his wiremill here.

The American sanitary industry was born in Trenton, the steel I-beams that made possible the skyscrapers of New York and Chicago were first rolled here, and the first American Belleek ware was made here. But while the industries spawned by those inventions were long the bedrock of a place sometimes known as "The City of Iron and Clay," a host of smaller concerns also found Trenton hospitable.

The most unusual may have been the oyster cracker industry, a huge business invented by English-born baker Adam Exton in 1847, when Americans ate oysters as freely as their descendants would eat ice cream. Some oyster crackers were eventually made elsewhere—the company had 30 imitators at one time—but they sold only if their bakers labeled them "Trenton crackers."

The pottery industry gave us not only china dinnerware and sanitary ware, but brickmakers and tilemakers and ceramic lampshade factories. Iron and steel contributed wire cable and bridge building, as well as makers of barbed-wire fences and manufacturers of all manner of machines. The rubber industry contributed a host of industrial products, as well as tires and linoleum.

What had been a boom town began to experience failures with the Depression, later accelerated here—as they were throughout the Northeast—by the availability of cheaper labor in the South. After World War II a number of large, family-held companies sold out to national corporations, paving the way for the later closing of outmoded Trenton plants. At the same time, however, the expansion of state government provided an important new source of jobs.

Some of the companies and organizations whose histories follow are survivors or offshoots of the boom years. Others are recent arrivals, lured by the same geographical factors that influenced our ancestors.

One of the solemn reminders of Trenton's role in World War I was the huge Victory Arch (built in 1918) on North Broad Street. The arch stood "to commemorate the patriotism of her sons who fought for liberty and right in the World War." Courtesy, Trentoniana Collection, TFPL

TRENTON HISTORICAL SOCIETY

The Eagle Tavern, built in 1765 as a residence and now maintained as a restaurant, was restored during the late 1970s by the Trenton Historical Society.

The Trenton Historical Society owes its existence to the Princes of Caliphs, an exotically named social organization begun in May 1902 as a branch of the local Knights of Malta. The Caliphs—who at one time had 1,200 members—adopted the custom of holding banquets to commemorate historic occasions.

William J. Backes, who served as chairman of the banquet committee for the Second Battle of Trenton observance on January 25, 1919, suggested the formation of a Trenton Historical Society at that dinner. At a meeting two months later, Chancellor Edwin R. Walker was elected the Society's first president.

The new group was instrumental in restoring the name of Mayor Frank

Members and their guests gather in an 18th-century room of the Eagle Tavern for the annual dinner of the Trenton Historical Society.

A. Magowan to the bronze plaque attached to the base of the Battle Monument. A progressive mayor from 1887 to 1889, Magowan later suffered personal and financial ruin and was quietly removed from the rolls of the monument's organizers. The Society's role was hailed by the *Trenton Sunday Advertiser* as a blow to "history faking."

Following the lead of one of its original trustees, John J. Cleary, the group's early causes included the campaign to save the home of Alexander Douglass, where Washington held his council of war during the Second Battle of Trenton. The Society sponsored the celebration of the 150th anniversary of the Battles of Trenton and took an active role in the observance of the city's sesquicentennial in 1929 by compiling a two-volume *History of Trenton*. Fifteen members wrote chapters and did the indexing for the authoritative work, whose first edition was sold to subscribers. A

second, one-volume edition was published by *The Trenton Times*, making the work a popular as well as a scholarly success.

The group's longtime interest in the preservation of city landmarks and historic sites is institutionalized in the ordinance establishing a landmarks commission, which the city adopted in 1972: At least two of the commission members must also hold membership in the Society.

Since the 1970s the Trenton Historical Society has devoted itself to the restoration of the Eagle Tavern as a historic landmark. Built in 1765 by the owner of the mills established by Mahlon Stacy and William Trent, the building at what is now 431-433 South Broad Street was a residence before its use as a tavern throughout the 19th century. In connection with the nearby Eagle Race Track, it was frequented by horse owners and served as a meeting place for South Ward politicians and members of the Eagle Fire Company. It became a boarding house at the turn of the century, but was vacant from 1947 until its acquisition by the city in 1965.

With the assistance of the city, county, state, and federal governments, the Society in the late 1970s undertook the $265,000 restoration of the property, which it leases from the city. Now listed on the state and national registers of historic places, it has been subleased since 1980 to a company which is committed to maintaining the Eagle Tavern as a working restaurant. The preservation of the group's headquarters and meeting place is its continuing concern.

GRIFFITH ELECTRIC SUPPLY COMPANY, INC.

The present location of Griffith Electric Supply Company, Inc., includes the original property on South Broad Street and several buildings on Second Street.

In 1938, when William S. and Meta A. Griffith began their wholesale electrical supply business, they had just one employee, John J. Rittmann. The three of them worked out of the Flatiron Building at 479 South Broad Street, with Bill Griffith out making the contacts, his wife running the showroom and doing the book-keeping, and Jack Rittmann at the counter.

Bill Griffith had started working for Trenton Electric at the age of 14, riding the trolley in from Pennington. While he never had the chance to attend high school, his employer paid for him to attend night technical classes at the School of Industrial Arts. Conscious of his lack of formal education, he was a lifelong student, a man who always had something to read when he got home from work.

The electrical business he began at the age of 31 was part of an industry growing at a tremendous rate. Determined to succeed, the Griffiths devoted their lives to their business, for years keeping their store open 60 or more hours a week and making deliveries in their Model A Ford— with electrical conduit hanging out of the windows. By 1940 they had a

full-time salesman, and within three years of starting out they were paying five employees.

Finding their downtown location accessible to customers and useful for delivery, the Griffiths never seriously considered moving to the suburbs. "Trenton has been good to us," Meta Griffith says, noting that the business has grown every year while being able to expand in its own neighborhood. In 1944 the Griffiths bought the property at 9 Second Street— previously used by the Margerum Provision Company—while continuing to rent across the way on South Broad Street. As bigger quarters were needed, they began buying adjacent properties—first, four houses at 13-19 Second Street, then those at 457-461, 485, and 495 South Broad Street, and 702 Bridge Street.

With the largest electrical distributorship inventory in the state, what began as a business with no more than 1,200 square feet now has 60,000 square feet of warehouse and office space, with 60 people employed in its current operations.

Seven early employees were given stock in the company in 1955. Following Bill Griffith's death in 1971, his wife became chairman of the board and secretary/treasurer and Jack Rittmann was made president of

the firm, which now counts 12 members in its shareholding management group.

The organization Meta Griffith heads is rated by the National Association of Electrical Distributors as the largest independent electrical supply company in the state and the 12th-largest single-house distributor in the country. But her work hasn't kept Meta Griffith from a host of activities. Active in the Mercer County Chamber of Commerce, as her husband was, in 1974 she became the first woman elected to the Chamber's board of directors and five years later was named the group's Citizen of the Year. She is presently serving as president of the Chamber.

William and Meta Griffith founded Griffith Electric Supply Company, Inc., in 1938 in this building at 479 South Broad Street.

SWITLIK PARACHUTE COMPANY, INC.

Amelia Earhart wearing a parachute manufactured by the Switlik Parachute Company as she returned from one of her record-breaking flights. Miss Earhart was the first woman to make a solo flight across the Atlantic Ocean.

In 1920, when Stanley Switlik bought the tiny Canvas-Leather Specialty Company at 241 South Warren Street, there were so few parachutes in use that no business anywhere depended on them. With his brother Walter, Switlik filled orders for mail pouches and tents, gradually adding flying suits and aviators' face masks—and even fur-lined suits for Admiral Byrd's first North Pole expedition.

In January 1927, four months before Lindbergh's solo flight across the Atlantic, the Switlik firm produced its own parachute design. Tested by the U.S. Navy the following year, it was found to be lighter, quicker opening, and slower descending than the model then in use. By 1931 the Army and Navy were ordering chutes from the newly renamed Switlik Parachute and Equipment Company.

But what should have been a prosperous era turned into a time of trial, with Stanley Switlik pursued by a series of patent suits brought by a rival. It cost $50,000 to win the suits, and the damage to his business forced him into reorganization in 1934.

Recovery was rapid: In September 1939 Switlik bought one of the old J.L. Mott warehouses at Lalor and Hancock streets, turning it into the world's largest parachute factory. By April 1940, 70 percent of all parachutes in use by the U.S. Armed Forces had been made by Switlik. By the end of 1943, when 95 percent of company facilities (including a second Mott warehouse) were devoted to war production, the work force had risen to an all-time high of 1,125 and was producing 1,900 parachutes weekly.

While the years immediately following the war were quieter, the Korean conflict put Switlik back in wartime production: Sales tripled from 1950 (when the company produced its 500,000th chute) to 1951. The postwar Switlik organization began to concentrate more on aviation and marine life rafts and life vests, and now produces more of them for the airlines of the world than any other company.

Like those who had preceded them, Vietnam fliers joined the Caterpillar Club, which is open to anyone who can present documentary proof that a parachute saved his life. Thousands of members have been sent their caterpillar pins since Switlik, which keeps members' stories on file, incorporated the club in 1943. Charles A. Lindbergh was the first to become a fourth-degree member, having survived four life-saving jumps.

Stanley and Wanda Switlik's children, Richard and Lottie, had joined the family firm during World War II and were named corporate officers after the war. In 1951 Richard replaced his father as president, adding responsibilities following Walter Switlik's death the next year, when the company moved into a new plant at 1325 East State Street.

A self-educated man—he arrived in this country from Poland at the age of 17—Stanley Switlik maintained a lifelong interest in education and conservation. He devoted himself increasingly to philanthropy from his partial retirement in 1962 until his death in 1981, deeding some 20,000 acres of undeveloped land to New Jersey, and aiding public schools and Rider College.

While the founders are gone, the family-owned business has plenty of talent to draw on. All three of Richard and Irene Switlik's sons, Richard Jr., Gregory, and Stanley, work at the Switlik Parachute Company.

A Switlik 46-person-capacity airline life raft is demonstrated in Germany to representatives of Lufthansa Airlines.

ST. FRANCIS MEDICAL CENTER

The main entrance to St. Francis Medical Center, 1983.

Three Sisters of St. Francis were sent from Glen Riddle, Pennsylvania, to Trenton in 1869. Led by Sister Mary Hyacintha, they were instructed not only to open a mission school at St. Francis Parish on Front Street, but also to explore the need for a hospital.

Four years after the end of the Civil War, there was still no place in the state capital where the sick and injured, infirm, or aged could go to receive medical care. From the small brick house they occupied at Market and Cooper streets, the Sisters of St. Francis began visiting the homes of the sick before and after their school day. When they had been in Trenton several months, they asked the Bishop of Newark for permission to start a hospital. Assured of the church's support, Sister Mary Hyacintha, Sister Mary Veronica, and Sister Mary Pancratia went out and begged for funds.

In 1870 they arranged to buy land at Hamilton Avenue and Chambers Street from Samuel K. Wilson, whose asking price was $1,800. The Sisters

could offer him only the $500 they had collected, which Wilson generously accepted as full payment. Work began the following fall, but the building proceeded slowly, as money was contributed. In January 1874 Sister Mary Hyacintha and two companions moved into the unfinished hospital, which was dedicated in May. The $38,000 building was described in the first annual report as "an imposing brick structure, 86 by 54 feet, with four stories and an attic." Ninety-eight patients were admitted to the 50 beds in 38 rooms during the first year.

Overcrowding was a problem almost from the beginning, so in 1888 the hospital purchased the rest of its block for $20,000, and in early 1903 Charles G. Roebling bought for $3,500 and gave to the hospital the land on Chambers Street and St. Francis Avenue as far back as Bert Avenue. Having gained the room for expansion, the hospital opened its first annex in 1896, when an operating room was also constructed. With the addition of a three-story wing in 1921, the bed capacity

totaled 225—but in 1924 alone, 4,450 patients were admitted. A nurses' residence was completed in 1925, when a building drive was started by the women of St. Francis' Aid, a group begun in 1916.

The hospital's modern history is one of steady expansion: a four-story brick wing in 1928, the eight-story North Wing in 1954 and School of Nursing Crean Hall three years later, the South Wing in 1964, and an addition to the North Wing in 1968. In the summer of 1974 the name was changed to St. Francis Medical Center, reflecting its certification as a teaching hospital affiliated with Hahnemann Medical College in Philadelphia. In 1982 a new clinical building and a new services building were completed.

Dedicated to the philosophy of its patron, St. Francis of Assisi, the medical center annually administers to some 40,000 patients—as residents and in clinic care—without regard to race, color, creed, sex, age, national origin, or financial status.

St. Francis Hospital as it appeared in the late 1800s.

TRANSAMERICA DELAVAL INC.

The impulse steam turbine invented by the Swedish Dr. Carl Gustav Patrik De Laval was first exhibited in this country at the World's Columbian Exposition at Chicago in 1893.

Scientific American devoted the cover of its edition of October 21, 1893, to illustrations of "De Laval's steam turbine developing a speed of 20,000 revolutions per minute, 20 horsepower," and eight views of the turbine and its parts. The story inside concluded that it "has proved itself superior to reciprocating steam engines." Three years later two units built by the De Laval Company of Stockholm were imported by New York Edison and became one of the first steam turbines to generate electricity in the United States.

With interest in this country assured, the De Laval Steam Turbine Company was formed with exclusive Western Hemisphere rights to the manufacture and sale of products associated with Dr. De Laval's invention. On October 18, 1900, the

Daily True American reported that an eight-acre Trenton site—"at the junction of the Pennsylvania railroad and the Trenton and Allentown turnpike, directly opposite the Rothschild's shirt factory"—had been chosen to produce steam turbines.

Employing 200 mechanics at the outset, the plant here shipped its first unit in 1902. In 1904, at the Louisiana Purchase Exposition, Dr. De Laval won the grand prize for the invention and development of the single-stage turbine and the company was awarded a gold medal for its centrifugal pumps. Both machines were more compact, easier to maintain, and had greater capacities than reciprocating equipment then in use.

The firm was already supplying machinery and equipment to the Navy by World War I, and during World War II its employment on war-related work caused its payroll to soar to 2,900 workers. Following the war, much of its work continued to be in ship propulsion machinery for the Navy's atomic-powered merchant ships and Polaris nuclear submarines. On the civilian side, De

The original 45,000-square-foot turbine plant in 1906.

Laval pioneered the use of centrifugal compressors for gas pipeline transmission.

As the work grew, the plant literally wore out. But De Laval's conservative foreign ownership refused to accept outside financing until 1962 when—having grown to the limit of its capital resources—the business was sold to an investment group. Transamerica, a San Francisco-based company, acquired the firm the following year and combined all of its manufacturing companies under the De Laval name, adopting the name Transamerica Delaval Inc. in 1978. Since Transamerica's ownership, the concern's facilities have been completely modernized.

The company now consists of 21 operating units in the United States, Canada, and Europe. Its specialized, precision-made engineered products range from machinery weighing as much as 100 tons to tiny switch sensors. The corporate headquarters is in Lawrence Township, with the Turbine and Compressor Division and the Delroyd Worm Gear Division both located in Hamilton Township, and the Condenser and Filter Division in Florence Township.

The Turbine and Compressor Division of Transamerica Delaval Inc. incorporates 670,000 square feet on a 100-acre site.

FREDERICK W. DONNELLY & SON

Four generations of Donnellys have served Trenton as men's clothiers, beginning in 1867 with Richard Augustus Donnelly. A Civil War veteran, General Donnelly served as New Jersey's quartermaster-general and was influential in having the state armory built here in 1903. He inaugurated a city institution by financing the first public concert in Cadwalader Park.

Busy with his many activities, the general welcomed his son, Frederick W., to the business in 1895. The younger man brought innovation with him, introducing a tailored-clothing department that was soon bigger than the original store. In 1903 father and son divided the business, with the R.A. Donnelly-named store remaining at the original site, on the ground floor of the Taylor Opera House, and F.W. Donnelly locating just down South Broad Street.

General Donnelly had been mayor of the city in 1884-1886, and in 1911 his son was elected to that office. A farsighted man, Mayor Donnelly served for 21 consecutive years. He supervised the store until his son, Frederick S., joined the family business in 1921, following naval aviation service in World War I. In 1927 the Frederick W. Donnelly & Son store moved to 35 East State Street, a four-story brick building then leased from the Katzenbach family. Three floors were devoted to selling—the first to men's haberdashery, hats, and shoes, the second to men's clothing, and the third to boys' clothing—while the fourth floor and basement served as stockrooms.

When Frederick S. Donnelly died in 1932 at the age of 35, his father resigned the mayor's office to supervise the business. Three years later, after Mayor Donnelly's own death at the age of 69, ownership of the family business passed to his daughters, Katherine Donnelly Haulenbeek and Helen Donnelly Hensler. Management of the store was shared by four longtime employees: Margaret Pickering, Larry Clark, George Rickard, and Jim Trumpore.

Frederick Donnelly Haulenbeek, grandson of F.W., joined the family store in 1950, becoming manager six years later as an expansion program put branch stores at the shore and in two Trenton suburbs. In 1971 Haulenbeek announced the closing of the downtown store and relocation to a new property, Lake Lawrence Plaza on Alternate Route 1 in Lawrence Township. Three years later, having worked for the company for 25 years, Haulenbeek purchased 100 percent of its corporate stock from other Donnelly family descendants.

In addition to merchandise made expressly for Frederick W. Donnelly

This photo was taken in the 1890s in front of Frederick W. Donnelly & Son.

& Son, the men's store's selection includes brand names long associated with it, such as H. Freeman, Hart Schaffner & Marx, Kingsridge, Corbin, Alden, and Pendleton. Haulenbeek, the fourth-generation owner, feels his family business succeeds as a specialty store due to its continuing quality and service. He points proudly to its long association with people such as Matt McNally, a 55-year employee; head tailor Tony Geronemo, a 40-year veteran; and Larry Clark, currently 46 years with the firm.

In 1903 this horse and carriage was the mode of transport for deliveries.

AMERICAN BILTRITE, INC.

In 1908 Miah Marcus and Frank Bernstein quit their jobs at a Massachusetts rubber company to start their own business in Trenton, armed with $5,000 each and their experience selling rubber heels and soles. Their gamble paid off right away, when the two men took orders for the annual capacity of their 200-square-foot factory on their first selling trip.

After World War I Robert G. Marcus, son of Miah, moved to Trenton to spearhead the development of a line of rubber flooring, matting, and stair treads, marketed as Amtico rubber flooring. The first major expansion didn't occur, however, until after World War II, when the company increased its production of rubber flooring tiles and, beginning in 1952, thermo-plastic vinyl flooring tiles.

The introduction of vinyl tiles revolutionized the resilient-flooring industry and led to continued expansion of the firm in the mid-1950s. It was during those years that Amtico pioneered the styling of a mass product for the whole industry by imitating the look of such natural textures as marble, wood, and flagstone. The first to introduce gold and other metallic designs in flooring, Amtico was also the first to emboss and valley print colored surface configurations.

In 1961 the company bought the Bonified Mills on East State Street in Hamilton Township, and with this facility developed the first embossed, in-register vinyl asbestos tile as well as the first urethane, no-wax tile. These and other innovations in design and technology permitted the expansion of the Bonified Mills plant, while continuing growth with existing products. The new plant more than doubled the flooring operation's capacity and sales.

The East State Street facility has remained the focus of the company's drive to use new technology in ways that have revolutionized the industry. In that process, Amtico has become one of the major manufacturers of resilient floor covering in the United States and is considered a leader in technological advances throughout its industry.

As recently as the early 1980s, Amtico again expanded with an entirely new production line that introduced the newest generation of resilient floor-covering products, under the trade names of Designer Carefree, Carefree, and Majestic. This latest expansion gives the company the ability to increase its production capacity by another 35 percent and further its market penetration.

What began as a two-man business is today a multimillion-dollar operation, with three major production lines in its East State Street plant and several satellite operations. Now publicly owned, the company is operated by the third generation of the Marcus family, which maintains a major interest in the corporation.

With more than 300,000 square feet of space in the Trenton area and a work force in excess of 300 people, American Biltrite is proud to have started here, stayed here, and maintained itself here for more than seven decades, and is proud of the large percentage of employees who have been with it for the past three decades.

American Biltrite's East State Street plant, acquired in 1961 from Bonified Mills, is the focus of the company's drive to use new technology. Expanded most recently in 1981, the plant has three major production lines.

HEINEMANN ELECTRIC COMPANY

Heinemann's circuit breaker testing area, circa 1960.

George Heinemann founded the Heinemann Electric Company in Philadelphia in 1888 as an electrical contracting business. The venture was incorporated in 1915, at which time B.S. Berlin became president and, subsequently, the principal stockholder.

In 1915 Heinemann began the manufacture of electrical cutout products in addition to continuing the contracting business. The manufacturing business soon eclipsed the contracting business, and the latter was discontinued.

In 1927 Berlin hired Kurt Wilckens of Hamburg, Germany, to direct the company's research program. Wilckens began experimenting with electrical circuit breakers and invented the hydraulic-magnetic circuit breaker, a design patented by Heinemann in 1934.

Needing more space, Heinemann in October 1929 moved next to New Jersey Porcelain's Plum Street plant in North Trenton. The relocation was advantageous to both concerns—

Heinemann's cutouts were housed in bases made by N.J. Porcelain.

The first Heinemann circuit breakers went on the market in 1930, when the company had only six employees in its circuit breaker department. Believing that its future growth would be made in sales of the new product, Heinemann began gradually phasing out cutout business in favor of making electrical protective devices. This trend was accelerated with the coming of World War II, because the airplane's new importance increased the need for magnetic circuit breakers.

In 1948 Heinemann engineers began work on electromagnetic relays, and by the late '50s the decision had been made to go after the specialty circuit breaker business. In 1957, as the firm was ending its porcelain-base fuse business, construction of the Trenton Freeway shut off expansion possibilities in its Plum Street neighborhood.

Bernard A. Berlin, who had succeeded his father as president after the latter's death in 1947, surveyed Heinemann employees before deciding on a new location. Convinced by their responses that the only acceptable location would be near their homes, "Barney" Berlin purchased property along the Brunswick Pike in Lawrence Township, a little more than two miles from the Plum Street plant. A building housing manufacturing facilities, main offices, research, development, and testing labs was dedicated there on September 6, 1960.

The younger Berlin died suddenly at the age of 49 in 1971, and was succeeded by his brother-in-law, Edgar Bromberg, a 35-year veteran of the company. Upon Bromberg's death four years later, James E. Shugars, who had been with Heinemann for 22 years, was named president.

Still a closely held enterprise, Heinemann today is the world's leading manufacturer of precision magnetic circuit breakers and solid-state relays. In addition to Trenton; Salisbury, Maryland; and Sanford, North Carolina, it maintains sales offices throughout the world and affiliated factories in Montreal, Melbourne, Geneva, and Johannesburg.

Heinemann circuit breakers are now a fixture even in space—where they have been used since the *Apollo 15* mission in 1971—and on *Skylab.*

Bernard A. Berlin at the dedication ceremonies on September 6, 1960, of the Heinemann Electric Company's facility on Brunswick Pike in Lawrence Township.

125

THE R.C. MAXWELL COMPANY

Billboards are an invention of the late 19th century, originally intended to attract the eye of railroad passengers. The success of the first ads painted on the sides and roofs of barns ensured that advertisers would want more space.

Robert Chester Maxwell, a 21-year-old sign painter, went into the new business in 1891. A one-man company, he had to locate places where billboards could be seen easily from trains, and then construct and paint the signs.

As the popularity of the automobile grew, rail passenger traffic declined and Maxwell and the helpers he'd begun hiring in the early years of this century transferred much of their business to roadside spots. With the commercial development of the incandescent bulb after World War I, electric display signs were added to their repertoire in 1919.

Maxwell, who saw great possibilities in these pedestrian-oriented "spectaculars," established

This was the corner of State and Broad streets before any signs were erected.

the Electric Sign Manufacturing Plant in Atlantic City. This subsidiary was responsible for such giant ads as the 50-foot Colgate thermometer, placed atop a Boardwalk building in the summer of 1922, when it was billed as the world's largest thermometer.

The firm's best-known ad was the one for Chesterfield cigarettes on Tilyou's Steeplechase Pier in Atlantic City. It was really two giant signs—each 215 feet in length and 55 feet in height—constructed back to back. Some 26,000 electric bulbs were installed when the sign was built in 1926, but the later addition of a new slogan, "Taste Above Everything," added another 1,000 bulbs. Four conduits, each six inches in diameter, were needed to supply the electricity for a load of 465,000 watts, or 465 kilowatts. The machinery necessary to produce the 75-second electric display was housed in a building 15 by 18 feet, hidden between the signs.

The company headquarters, located at 147 East State Street until 1910, moved to 143-147 East Front

Street and then to State and Broad before ending up at 413 East State Street in 1915. In August 1932 The R.C. Maxwell Company bought out the Trenton Advertising Company and its subsidiaries, the Trenton Poster Advertising Company and the Trenton Outdoor Advertising Company, moving into that firm's building at 725 East State Street, where it remains.

It was during R.C. Maxwell's presidency of the Trenton Chamber of Commerce that the Chamber's *Trenton* magazine was born in 1924. The advertising executive also devoted a great deal of time to the local chapter of the American Red Cross, of which he was president many times. Following his 1954 death, his widow became president of the family firm, and was succeeded by George Harvey, Jr. Joseph B. Ringkamp was named president in 1965 and retired two years later when the founder's son, David Maxwell, took over.

The R. C. Maxwell Company owns over 1,000 billboards and builds several new ones annually. Its 60 employees, who operate in Mercer, Burlington, Bucks, Cape May, and Atlantic counties, can justly claim to work for a firm that's as old as its industry.

The R.C. Maxwell Company's signs provided the corner with a lively look after World War I.

ROLLER BEARING COMPANY OF AMERICA

Families, friends, good fortune: These three ingredients comprise the factors that have ensured the success of RBC for the past 63 years and that of other Trainer family enterprises for the past 120 years. Incorporated in 1920, RBC was fortunately attracted to Trenton in 1928 by the then-secretary of the Trenton Chamber of Commerce, Walter O. Lochner, and the new Industries Committee of the Chamber, headed by Frank J. Wetzel, chairman. Thanks to these gentlemen and their dedication to Trenton, the move was effected from Newark. A front-page story in *The Trenton Times* on March 30, 1928, quotes Joseph C. Trainer, president, as saying "his company [RBC] will become a leading industry in Trenton." Today the firm continues to believe that these words were both prophetic and accurate.

Trenton, through its long history, has been a city of closely knit families. The Mercer automobile company was owned principally by the Roebling and Kuser families, who manufactured this fine car at the Whitehead Road site. When it was purchased by the Trainer family, many of the technically oriented employees joined the new venture, turning their skills to the manufacture of precision bearings. There is a fine heritage of father-and-son relationships continuing to this day.

Survival through the troubled '30s can be summed up in one word— friends. Through the cooperation of the late Governor Stokes and Harold Ray of the First Mechanics National Bank, and the late Messrs. John A. Campbell and Caleb Green of the

The Mercer Automobile Company plant as it looked in 1928, when Roller Bearing Company of America moved to Trenton and purchased it.

Trenton Banking Company, financing was made possible. RBC completed the move from Newark in late 1928, one year before the stock market crash of 1929. It was clear by 1934 that RBC had more manufacturing space than it needed. The Thermoid Company, owned by the Schluter family, was located on the opposite side of Whitehead Road. Their president was Fred Schluter and vice-president was the late William Pardoe. They were in need of additional space, and the total property was sold to Thermoid and part leased back. It is important to note that during this period Thermoid sorely needed the RBC area, but through the kindness of Schluter and Pardoe, RBC was never disturbed. This act of true friendship made survival possible.

By December 1952 RBC had outgrown the Whitehead Road facility, and through the help of the First Mechanics National Bank, in the persons of Sidney Stevens and Richard Macgill, financing was arranged permitting Arthur D. Rogers, architect, and the Simon Belli contracting firm to build the first structure on Sullivan Way.

Happily, attitudes remain much the same today. Ed Meara, executive director of the Mercer County Chamber of Commerce, follows in the footsteps of his predecessors by offering ongoing aid and assistance. RBC continues, knowing that with a little bit of luck, old friends, and the continuity of families, success is ensured.

Today the headquarters of the Roller Bearing Company of America is on Sullivan Way in West Trenton.

NEW JERSEY NATIONAL BANK

The Trenton Banking Company's 1838 banking house became known as the "Marble Bank." New Jersey National Bank is a direct descendant of this institution.

The site of the main office of New Jersey National Bank at 1 West State Street is a landmark of city, state, and national importance.

A stone-and-stucco hostelry, called at various times "Thirteen States,"

In 1930 The First-Mechanics National Bank completed and dedicated its banking house on "The Corner Historic."

"French Arms," "Blazing Star," and "City Tavern," was built in 1730 on the southwest corner of King (Warren) and Second (State) streets. It first hosted sessions of New Jersey's House of Assembly in 1780, and welcomed the Continental Congress on Monday, November 1, 1784.

It was there, in the tavern's Long Room, that Congress bade farewell to General Lafayette on December 10, 1784, presenting him with a sealed envelope to be delivered personally to "The Honorable Benjamin Franklin, Minister Plenipotentiary of the United States to France." It was there, on December 18, 1787, that all 39 delegates to the state legislature voted to ratify the new Constitution of the United States. And it was there, on April 20, 1789, that General Washington, on his way to New York to be inaugurated, sat down to dinner with the town's leading citizens following his public reception at the Assunpink.

No doubt because it was still the city's biggest public meeting space, it was to the Long Room of the City Tavern at 10 a.m. on Tuesday, January 8, 1805, that the Trenton Banking Company invited those interested in buying its stock. Just a month earlier, the General Assembly had passed "An act to erect and establish a Banking Company in the city of Trenton."

The city's second bank also traces its roots to the tavern, where on December 23, 1832, a mass meeting was called to petition the legislature for the chartering of the Mechanics and Manufacturers Bank.

Both banks located within a block of the tavern and when, in 1836, bigger quarters were needed by Mechanics and Manufacturers, its directors authorized the purchase of the corner tavern property. The century-old City Tavern was razed and a two-story brick building with a slate roof put in its place, at a cost of $3,500. The new bank was completed in 1837, two years before the Trenton Banking Company opened its own new quarters on the site of the old Hunterdon County Court House, just around the corner on Warren Street.

But 1837 is remembered less for building plans than for its financial crisis, caused by the proliferation of under-capitalized banks. Both Trenton banks withstood the Panic of 1837 and a similar one in 1857. Following the adoption of the National Banking Act of 1864—which created a national currency and provided for the issuance of national charters to banks that could meet capitalization requirements— Mechanics and Manufacturers Bank received such a charter and, in 1865, changed its name to Mechanics National Bank.

In 1928 Mechanics National Bank undertook the first of what was to become a series of mergers with competitors. After its merger with First National Bank of Trenton, which had been chartered in 1864, the new bank was known as The First-Mechanics National Bank of Trenton.

Following the stock market crash of 1929, a number of small city banking institutions began to experience problems. One result was that both the Chambersburg Trust Company and the Wilbur Trust Company were absorbed by The First-Mechanics National Bank in August 1931.

Its considerable growth led the bank to plan a replacement of its original building on the tavern site. Designed to convey strength, stability, and security at a time when bank customers understandably lacked faith in financial institutions, the building's marble and limestone facade hides underpinnings of structural steel.

The West State Street cornice bears the legend, "The Corner Historic," to commemorate its place in history. Inside, the ceilings of the main banking room soar to a level three stories above the floor, while the wall opposite the front doors boasts a mural of George Washington by illustrator W.C. Wyeth, father of painter Andrew Wyeth.

In 1958 the Trenton Banking Company and The First-Mechanics National Bank of Trenton consolidated to form First Trenton National Bank, the sixth-largest banking institution in the state and the largest in Central Jersey. Harvey C. Emery was named chairman of the board and Sydney G. Stevens became president.

The new bank acquired the Hightstown Trust Company in 1964 and the Lambertville National Bank five years later, giving it a total of 13 banking offices.

Its 1970 merger with New Jersey National Bank and Trust Company, headquartered in Monmouth County, made it the state's fifth-largest bank and changed its name to the one still used—New Jersey National Bank. Led by chairman Sydney G. Stevens, vice-chairman Joseph Thummess, and president Richard G. Macgill, the shareholders of the new institution voted to form a bank holding company known as New Jersey National Corporation, in

order to organize new banks and acquire bank-related businesses.

The corporation opened the first of these, the New Jersey National Bank of Princeton, and acquired the Underwood Mortgage and Title Company, the third-largest mortgage firm based in New Jersey, in 1973. The Delaware Valley National Bank of Cherry Hill was acquired the following year.

In December of the bicentennial year, New Jersey National Corporation passed the billion-dollar mark in assets as John H. Walther and John D. Wallace were appointed chairman and president, respectively. That same month saw the purchase of the First State Bank of Toms River.

With 52 branches in nine counties, the modern New Jersey National Bank bears little resemblance to its ancestors. But within bank headquarters at the Corner Historic, the Washington mural watches over a distinguished heritage.

John H. Walther, chairman of the board of New Jersey National Corporation and New Jersey National Bank.

John D. Wallace, president of New Jersey National Corporation and New Jersey National Bank.

BASE TEN SYSTEMS, INC.

Base Ten Systems' 61,600-square-foot facility located in Hamilton Township.

In January 1966 three electronics engineers working at a Princeton firm decided to start their own company to provide electronics hardware for use in military aircraft.

Myles M. Kranzler, William M. Errickson, and James A. Eby had known each other since the 1950s and often talked of their own business. Together they raised $200,000, hired a secretary and one other engineer, and plunged into the highly competitive world of international avionics contracting.

The fledgling enterprise in 1967 developed flight test instrumentation for the *Apollo* spacecraft which first carried man to the moon, following that up with contracts for data gathering and encoding systems to assist pilots of the U.S. Navy and Air Force.

But by 1975, with most of its defense contracts completed and no new airplane development planned in the United States, the company faced a crisis. The work week was cut back to four days and management took a pay cut in order to hold its

engineering team together while bidding on a Stores Management System for the West German version of NATO's all-purpose fighter plane, the Tornado. In February 1976 Base Ten—whose biggest previous year had seen total sales of $3 million—was awarded a single contract of almost $3 million for the development of this Stores Management System. When all Tornado manufacturing contracts end in the 1990s, corporate revenues from them will have exceeded $100 million.

While the company achieved major growth by concentrating on microprocessor circuit and software design for defense clients, it has more recently applied the know-how and capital accumulated from those systems to the telephone industry.

The technology used in Base Ten's aircraft weapons systems has been adapted to provide fire, burglary, and other alarm-reporting equipment for sale to telephone companies. A small terminal installed in a home or business receives information from sensors located at the site, transmitting it over existing telephone lines to a central computer. The sensors are automatically scanned once a minute and the information is received by computer whether or not the phone is in use. Already in place in Canada, it is being tested by U.S.

telephone companies.

Weapon control systems are the principal products of the firm's wholly owned subsidiary, Base Ten Systems, Ltd., of Farnborough, England, which employs almost 100 people; Base Ten Systems Electronics GmbH has a staff of 60 in Munich to provide manufacturing, sales, and technical support for company products sold in Germany; and the venture's newest addition, Base Ten of Canada, Ltd., supports the maintenance and field service of alarm-reporting systems sold in Canada.

Located on 16 acres of land in Hamilton Township, where almost 300 workers are now employed, Base Ten in 1982 added 26,600 square feet of floor area to the 35,000 square feet it already occupied.

Myles M. Kranzler, who is both president and chairman of the board, points with pride to the incentive program that gives employees a half-percent salary increase for each one-percent gain in corporate productivity. Base Ten, which has enjoyed such rapid growth in its less than 20 years of existence, looks confidently to the future.

The circled inset identifies typically installed Base Ten avionics equipment aboard a high-performance jet fighter aircraft.

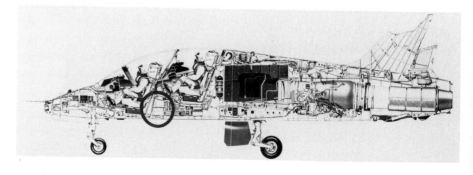

HELENE FULD MEDICAL CENTER

On the evening of March 10, 1887, six city doctors interested in establishing a homeopathic dispensary met at the 6 North Stockton Street home of Wilson Pierson. The Trenton City Dispensary, which Drs. F.H. Williams, James R. Cooper, Eugene B. Witte, William T. Rogers, William G. McCullough, and William H. Griffin opened at that address, was a one-room affair.

Two years later this board purchased the farmhouse and six acres of land on Brunswick Avenue from the estate of dairy farmer Samuel E. DeCou. The furnished house, which had been Miss Anna DeCou's private school, was dedicated as the Trenton City Hospital on June 6, 1889, and opened as a 25-bed institution that November.

Knowing larger quarters were needed, the board began a fund drive in 1900. A four-story brick and stone building was finished in September 1902 and renamed the William McKinley Memorial Hospital to

In its 97th year of service to the city, the Helene Fuld Medical Center presents a new facade to Brunswick Avenue.

honor the assassinated president. The old farmhouse continued in service as the residence of women enrolled in the hospital's Training School for Nurses, which opened on October 22, 1890, as the city's first nursing school.

The 1902 annual report indicates that 449 patients were admitted that year, nearly double the 1901 number. The dispensary handled 2,636 cases—all but a few of them charity patients—some 70 percent of whom required surgery. "Although much has been done, there is still much to do," the report concluded, noting that the Ladies' Association planned to install a new laundry and paint the old hospital building, while the Benevolent Association of the Secret Orders would soon buy "a horse and harness suitable for the ambulance."

On Henry C. Kelsey's death in 1919, the hospital received a bequest of $50,000 for the construction of a new nurses' residence, built on the northwest corner of the property. In 1924, and again in 1948, major hospital additions and improvements were undertaken.

Beginning in the 1950s, Dr. Leonhard Felix Fuld provided the means for construction of new nursing school buildings and patient care areas. The Helene Fuld Health Foundation, named for his mother,

was the donor, and in 1960 the hospital's name was changed to Helene Fuld. The full name has been Helene Fuld Medical Center since 1972.

The 1976 addition of the Gordon A. Philips Critical Care Pavilion combined intensive care, coronary care, and progressive care in one facility. Fully accredited, the medical center was designated a teaching hospital in 1974, affiliated with Philadelphia's Hahnemann Medical College. It serves as the communications and administrative headquarters for the Mercer County Mobile Intensive Care Program, and is the regional dialysis center for Mercer, Hunterdon, and parts of Burlington, Warren, and Lower Bucks counties.

Eighty years after completion of its first building on Brunswick Avenue, work was finished on a $14-million project which relocated 80 of the medical center's 375 beds, expanded the surgery, laboratory, radiology, admissions, and emergency departments, and relocated the School of Nursing to 832 Brunswick Avenue. Helene Fuld Medical Center now presents a new facade to the city it has served for 97 years.

In the 1890s graduate nurses surround the director of the Training School for Nurses, Trenton's first nursing school. In the background is the DeCou farmhouse, the first home of the Trenton City Hospital.

H.M. ROYAL, INCORPORATED

H.M. Royal is a second-generation rubber man whose father worked for the Home Rubber Company and whose mother was a member of the Stokes family, owners of both Home Rubber Company and Joseph Stokes Rubber Company. The young man founded H.M. Royal, Incorporated, on October 25, 1925.

Royal was attracted to the supplying of raw materials to the rubber industry with its heavy concentration in the Trenton area. Early distribution was done within 10 to 15 miles of the city. The southward movement of the rubber industry has caused the company to expand its operations. Its Trenton office services an area east of the Mississippi; a Downey, California, office services the West Coast; and a Spartanburg, South Carolina, office services the Southeast.

In the beginning Royal had the help of just one male worker and one female clerk. Today, as the firm's chairman of the board, he is joined in the administration of the family-owned business by his three sons— H.M. Royal III, president; H.L. Boyer Royal, senior vice-president/ sales; and Toms B. Royal, senior vice-president/technical matters. The firm now employs from 50 to 60 people, with 27 office staff members in Trenton, Downey, and Spartanburg.

The company specializes in the distribution of mineral products— clays, talc, and calcium carbonates used as fillers and extenders. In addition, it emphasizes the sale and distribution of sulfur for industrial and rubber purposes. Many of the products Royal markets have been made to its specification and are sold

under its names, although it also acts as a distributor of others' products and as a manufacturers' agent.

In 1933 the firm moved to its present location at 689 Pennington Avenue. The early existing buildings, which have been modified and expanded, are decorated with deep-sea fishing trophies won by H.M. Royal and also boast one stained-glass marlin among the lead-glass panels in his office windows overlooking Norman Avenue.

H.M. Royal, Incorporated, located opposite the city reservoir, has grown over the years, with a large warehouse addition built in 1977 for the storage and handling of chemicals and manufacturers' raw materials. The company leases a fleet of tractors and trailers, whose garage and repair facility is at this location.

Over the years, H.M. Royal, Incorporated, has stayed with the same product lines, expanding and changing suppliers and reaching out to take advantage of changing geography. Two of the founder's grandsons have joined the firm as it

H.M. Royal, Incorporated, is located at 689 Pennington Avenue, Trenton.

approaches its 60th anniversary, still very much a part of the rubber industry.

Founded in 1925, H.M. Royal, Incorporated, approaches its 60th anniversary still very much a part of the rubber industry.

TRENTON SHEET METAL, INC.

Frederick F. Scheich, an Austro-Hungarian immigrant who had been trained as a tinsmith in his homeland, began his own business in the basement of his house at 408 Rutherford Avenue in 1912. He used a bicycle to get to jobs and deliver materials until, in 1915, he needed bigger quarters and a car. Five years later he moved again, to 30 Adam Avenue, where the business is still located.

By the 1920s his company was one of the area's largest sheet metal houses, employing as many as 200 men in work on Trenton's City Hall, the YMCA and YWCA, junior high schools 3 and 4, Trenton Central High, the State House Annex, the War Memorial, and the marquees of the Lincoln, Capitol, Greenwood, and Olden movie theaters.

Scheich expanded in 1927 by setting up the Trenton Sheet Metal Supply House for the sale of building and maintenance supplies. But as the Depression deepened, the company was forced to change its focus from large contract installations to specialty design and fabricating work.

Following the founder's death in 1949, his widow and daughter sold a part interest to four partners in 1951: George L. Fluck, Joseph P. Somogyi, Russell H. Bogert, and John B. Cole, Sr. Six years later Fluck retired, and the remaining three partners bought his share and that of the Scheich family. Since 1963 the firm has been entirely owned by the Somogyi family.

Joseph Somogyi, whose mother was a cleaning woman for the Scheichs, joined the firm in 1924, at the age of 14. He worked for three years as a helper until there was an opening for him in a five-year apprenticeship. Encouraged by his employer, Somogyi studied at night to get a high school diploma and also took courses at the School of Industrial Arts. By 1939, when Scheich decided to retire, the younger man was running the business much of the time.

Trenton Sheet Metal is a custom producer of everything from commercial ventilating systems to Ocean Spray cranberry tanks, and its jobs reflect the changes in the city. During the '30s and '40s, when Trenton was still a manufacturing center, the company never went beyond city limits for work. Now its employees travel for jobs that range in complexity from covering church spires in copper to making component parts for nuclear plants.

Joseph P. Somogyi (center), who retired in 1972, was succeeded by his sons, Raymond (left), vice-president, and Robert (right), president of Trenton Sheet Metal, Inc.

When the elder Somogyi retired in 1972, his sons, Robert and Raymond, split the running of the company; Robert, the president, looks after installations, while his younger brother, the vice-president, handles the shop work. Marilyn Somogyi, Robert's wife, is the firm's secretary/treasurer. Since the 1940s Trenton Sheet Metal's size has remained the same. It still employs 35 workers, five in the office.

The company fabricates in all kinds of metal and does all types of welding; it will form, shear, and roll-shear a sheet of metal up to 3/8-inch thick, and cut metal to patterns of any size and shape. While most of its work is industrial, the company has long worked with artists and inventors, producing sculpture as well as prototype machinery.

Citing their own experience as well as that of Fred Scheich and their father, the Somogyi brothers say no job is too small for Trenton Sheet Metal, nor is any customized job too large.

133

NEW JERSEY BELL

Trenton took to the telephone early—in 1879, just three years after Alexander Graham Bell unveiled his "talking toy."

The town's first telephone wires were run from a switchboard in the Continental Telegraph office at 32 Greene (Broad) Street. W. Scott Taylor had the first phone installed in his drugstore on Perry Street, near Greene. Other pioneer customers included Mercer Rubber, Wilson's Wool Mill, and Moore's Pottery.

The first directory, published in 1880, included the names of Mayor Frank A. Magowan; John L. Murphy, publisher of the *State Gazette;* and Peter Katzenbach, owner of the Trenton House and the American House hotels. By the following year 125 subscribers were listed—an increase of more than 100.

With that much business, the telegraph office manager was unable to handle all the calls. Richard Van Horne was the first operator to be hired in 1881 for a shift during full-time hours. Women began to be hired several years later. Trenton was the first city near Philadelphia to employ women as night operators.

Starting in 1882, calls could be made outside the city, thanks to a single iron wire run to Yardville in June and to Bordentown in October. During the next two years, lines were placed between Trenton and Lawrenceville and Princeton.

A number of telephone companies operated in Trenton well into the 1900s. Included were the Trenton Telephone Company, the Delaware and Atlantic Telegraph and Telephone Company, the Home Telephone Company of Trenton,

Operators at an 1887 switchboard.

and the Fayette Home Telephone Company.

In 1899 a three-story brick building at 216 East State Street became the headquarters of the Delaware and Atlantic Telegraph and Telephone Company. Built on the site where Hessian soldiers surrendered after the first Battle of Trenton, it was replaced by a five-story building in 1914.

A decade later three more floors were added and a wing built to house future dial equipment. New Jersey Bell was formed on October 1, 1927.

The first dial equipment was installed in the late 1920s. In 1930 Trenton became the second city in the state to convert completely to dial service. Another city milestone occurred in 1968, when an Electronic Switching System office with 43,000 lines—then the largest

in the country—went into service.

Mercer County now has about 1,600 New Jersey Bell employees serving some 333,500 telephones. AT&T Long Lines and Western Electric employ another 600 in the county.

Almost a century later, operators work at highly automated call processors.

AMERICAN DECORATORS, INC.

In the late 1930s, when most American lamps were made with ceramic bases, the dinnerware decorating work of the Firth Studio in Indianapolis impressed a New York manufacturer, Lulis Lamp Company, which tried to hire Clarence Firth. He agreed to relocate in the East and in 1939 came to Trenton to work at the Croydon China Company along with his sons, Clarence Jr. and John R., in back of the Bay Ridge Pottery, near the reservoir.

America's entry into World War II stopped the importing of glass, wood, and brass lamp bases and created a boom in the manufacture of ceramic ones. But while the production of ceramics could be increased, their decorating by hand remained a time-consuming process. Faced with an immediate need, the owners of Lulis offered to put up the money if Clarence Firth would open a shop.

He called it 15 Coates Street Corporation, after its location in the former factory of Capitol Bedding Company at that address. The first kiln was fired there on August 26, 1944, with Firth joined by his son, Clarence Jr.; Laura Moffett, a freelance artist who was the first person hired; and two other hand decorators. Working for Rembrandt, Stiffel and Crest, as well as Lulis, the firm's artists talked over designs with the manufacturers' representatives. At the height of the demand for hand-decorated ware, the company employed 38 workers.

But with war's end, work dropped off as imports returned. John joined the firm in January 1946 upon his

Clarence Firth, Jr., unloads a kiln filled with lamp bases in 1944.

discharge from the service. His father died the following November, and Clarence Jr. and John decided to expand at that time. Clarence designed and built a 30-foot tunnel kiln, enlarging the old mattress factory in 1947-1948. American Decorators continued to do lamp work but, with those orders slowing, began to concentrate on promotional items for business.

Firth and Laura Moffett had married in 1951, and she suggested they try the college market. They went out and called on 50 colleges, and sold all of them. A petite blonde who called herself a traveling saleswoman for beer mugs, she eventually lined up sales representatives willing to carry American Decorators' college line. In addition to that work, the firm decorated sanitary ware in the '50s and '60s for Rheem Manufacturing Company of Metuchen.

The Firth family built its tiny company into the largest supplier of decorated ceramics to the college market: 900 colleges and universities now buy from the firm, through its 15 sales representatives. Following her husband's death in 1977, Mrs. Firth and her brother-in-law have carried on the business, whose 11 employees annually decorate and ship their specialized ceramic ware throughout the country.

Tankards, coffee mugs, and plates decorated with college seals are the staple, but fraternities, naval ships, and commercial enterprises are also steady customers. Once seasonal, the college business has become a year-round one, although fall and spring are still the busiest times, as new students and new graduates look for mementos.

Founder Clarence Firth, Sr., in a 1946 photo.

RIDER COLLEGE

Founded in 1865 as the Trenton Business College, the educational institution that became Rider College grew and was nurtured within the Trenton community for nearly a century.

At the close of the Civil War, the newly established Trenton Business College (part of the Bryant-Stratton chain) engaged the "main saloon" of Temperance Hall, on the southeast corner of Broad and Front streets, for $50 a month. The curriculum consisted of arithmetic, business ethics, bookkeeping, general office management, telegraphy, and penmanship.

Andrew J. Rider, a teacher with Bryant-Stratton in Newark, became principal (and later acquired ownership) of the Trenton school in 1866. That same year a "ladies' department" was added, and the school relocated to a larger facility at 20-22 East State Street. Successive moves were to the Masonic Temple, corner of State and Warren, in 1885; and the Ribsam Building, Broad and Front streets, in 1896.

Rider, who served in the state legislature and became known as "the cranberry king of South Jersey," sold the school to Franklin B. Moore in 1898. At the dawn of the 20th century, the school was merged with another private enterprise in Trenton, the Stewart School of Business, owned by John E. Gill.

The Rider-Moore and Stewart School of Business flourished. In 1921 the school officially became Rider College and moved into a newly constructed four-story building at the corner of East State and Carroll streets, where it remained for 43 years. By the time Rider was authorized to grant its first undergraduate degree in 1922 and its first graduate degree in 1927, the principal components of the college's present-day configuration were in place: It was coeducational and nonsectarian; students could attend full or part time, day and evening; and it offered courses in business, liberal arts and sciences, and education.

What was once a small business school had grown into a highly respected, multipurpose, nonprofit institution of higher learning. By the mid-'50s the physical plant consisted of 17 buildings scattered throughout the city. To consolidate the college's facilities and unify the student body, the decision was made to seek a single tract of land. In 1965 Rider completed the move to its present 340-acre campus in suburban Lawrence Township.

By 1981 the college's enrollment was 3,350 full-time and 1,500 part-time undergraduates, plus some 1,000 graduate students. There are 35 modern buildings (including 27 student residences) in close proximity to athletic fields, and a lake. Cornerstones of the academic program are a highly qualified faculty, a 350,000-volume library, and a sophisticated computer network.

The college's progress has been built upon the solid foundation established in 1865. Rider takes pride in its past as it plans for an exciting future as part of the greater Trenton community.

Rider College's classroom and library buildings were located at East State and Carroll streets until 1965.

Andrew J. Rider, former owner of the Trenton Business College.

SONIC INSTRUMENTS

Ultrasonic nondestructive testing is an industry that dates only to the industrial expansion that followed World War II. Used originally for routine maintenance, these precision testers and monitoring devices are now employed in extremely complex, integrated high-speed inspection systems for the aerospace, marine, ordnance, nuclear, chemical and petrochemical, construction, automotive, and metal and plastic fabrications industries.

Sonic Instruments is located at 1014 Whitehead Road Extension, Trenton.

into a larger space in the Ewing Business Park on Whitehead Road Extension.

Much of Sonic's growth is attributable to its reputation as a style-setter whose designs have followed the needs of industry somewhat more quickly than its competitors. The marketplace for Sonic designs is with any industry that creates and manufactures critical goods. Its equipment is used for a product in stress situations, the majority being metal goods, although plastics and woods comprise a small section of the business.

began construction on a one-story, 20,000-square-foot building at 1014 Whitehead Road Extension, adjacent to the leased plant. The additional space enabled the company to expand its operation for a product line which now includes devices used for engineering, quality control, product assurance, qualification, material evaluation, production control, inspection, and maintenance. With $7 million in annual sales and 110 employees, Sonic Instruments is now ranked second in a field of six similar companies.

John S. Oliano, president of Sonic Instruments.

Looking at the three significant companies in the field in the late 1960s, John Oliano saw areas where competition was possible. He incorporated Sonic in April 1969 to manufacture and market ultrasonic test instruments for use in process control, quality control, and material inspection.

The first plant was a small building at Mercer County Airport, where the new business grew steadily, at least 10 percent a year and some years 20 percent. By 1975 the company had outgrown its quarters and moved

After a study of needs by the company's application engineers, its technical services group determines whether a client's needs can be met with basic equipment or by modifying existing components. If not, Sonic design engineers will design a special instrument or system to meet the specific test requirements. The firm conducts technical seminars and training programs to ensure that the customer's employees understand how to set up, operate, and maintain the new equipment.

Ten years after its founding, Sonic

The firm boasts an international list of clients; automotive customers alone include Chrysler, Fiat, Ford, General Motors, and Volvo. In March 1982 Sonic was acquired by Staveley Industries, an English conglomerate. As a wholly owned subsidiary, with John Oliano continuing as president, Sonic Instruments looks forward to further expansion of its international markets.

MERCER COUNTY COMMUNITY COLLEGE

Because the Centennial Exposition awakened Americans to the threat of foreign competition, the New Jersey State Legislature in the 1880s encouraged industrial training. In Trenton, an Evening Drawing School began workers' classes in 1890.

With the support of workers from John A. Roebling's Sons Company and the Potters' Association, the school board agreed in 1898 to an expanded Trenton Technical School of Science and Art at 120 North Broad Street—with 31 students in free-hand drawing and 26 in mechanical drawing. In 1901 the renamed School of Industrial Arts moved to 219 East State Street. There were three instructional departments: art, applied art, and mechanical drawing.

Henry Cooper Kelsey, a Trenton banker who served as New Jersey's secretary of state, announced in 1909 that he would finance a new school as a memorial to his wife, Prudence Townsend Kelsey. He spent $142,000 to erect a Florentine palazzo-style building at the corner of Willow and West State streets.

Art had been stressed until the school's 1911 move to the Kelsey Building, which made day classes and expanded technical curricula possible. Upon director Frank F. Frederick's death in 1952, the enrollment was 1,266—five times what it was when the fourth director took office in 1906.

In 1947 the school became Trenton Junior College, with curricula in engineering and art. Henry J. Parcinski, the engineering director, became college president in 1948 and, while maintaining the art program, he greatly expanded engineering and introduced programs in liberal arts and science.

Much as an earlier legislature had encouraged the creation of technical schools, so in 1962 the legislature passed a measure governing the establishment and operation of county colleges. The Mercer County Board of Chosen Freeholders appointed a study commission, which advised a county referendum. Passed overwhelmingly, the referendum led to the January 11, 1966, establishment of Mercer County Community College.

Dr. Richard K. Greenfield was appointed president, overseeing the merger with Trenton Junior College in 1967. A 300-acre site in West Windsor and Hamilton townships was chosen, and groundbreaking for the $22-million campus took place in 1969.

When the new campus opened in the summer of 1972, the Kelsey Building was sold to the state but leased back to the college as its temporary Trenton center. The James Kerney Foundation funded the college's 1974 purchase of land on

The James Kerney Center in downtown Trenton is the main campus of Mercer County Community College.

North Broad Street, near the home of the original Trenton Technical School of Science and Art. The James Kerney Campus was dedicated there in the spring of 1975, the year that John P. Hanley succeeded Dr. Greenfield as president.

The main campus, James Kerney Campus, and other off-campus centers are now attended by 14,000 full- and part-time students who are enrolled in more than 70 one- and two-year curricula in addition to a wide variety of community education and training programs.

Mercer County Community College's West Windsor Campus Quadrangle is situated on 300 acres in West Windsor and Hamilton townships.

PITMAN-MOORE, INC.

Harry C. Pitman and John C. Myers pooled their savings in Indianapolis in 1899 and began their own business in a one-room store. With assets of less than $5,000, the young drug salesmen called on doctors and drugstores by day, filling and packing orders with their wives' help at night.

They were successful enough to move, in 1905, to a much larger building opposite the Indiana State House. When Myers left the firm several years later, an employee named Harry Moore became president and the Pitman-Myers Company became the Pitman-Moore Company.

In 1929 Pitman-Moore joined four other serum-producing firms to form Allied Laboratories, Inc. During World War II the company was a major supplier of influenza vaccine to the military, in what is believed to be the largest-scale clinical evaluation of a product ever known.

The construction in 1912 of a complex of biological laboratories outside of Indianapolis had given the fledgling enterprise the ability to invest its resources in greater research and the development of new products. Pitman-Moore played an early and important role in the commercial production of gamma globulin, which is capable of modifying or preventing measles and infectious hepatitis, and in 1955 the firm was one of five to produce and distribute large quantities of Salk polio vaccine.

In 1960 Allied and Pitman-Moore merged with the Dow Chemical Company of Midland, Michigan, one of the country's largest chemical firms. In March 1969 the Veterinary Division, its products, and the name Pitman-Moore were sold by Dow to Johnson & Johnson. Harry W. McNey, president of McNeil Laboratories, also assumed the presidency of Pitman-Moore, whose laboratories and business offices were temporarily housed at McNeil's Fort Washington, Pennsylvania, headquarters.

With the addition of surgical products and drugs developed by other Johnson & Johnson companies, Pitman-Moore rapidly expanded its own line to become the leading broad-line producer of ethical veterinary drugs and supplies. Since its acquisition as a wholly owned subsidiary of Johnson & Johnson, the organization has also expanded its line each year as an outgrowth of its own research. Pitman-Moore points proudly to such firsts as the isolation of infectious bovine rhinotracheitis virus; the infectious canine hepatitis tissue culture vaccine; the first licensed tissue culture canine distemper vaccine; the feline rhinotracheitis vaccine; the feline calicivirus vaccine; and the clinical chemistry system based on animal blood values.

The employer of 130 people when it was acquired by Johnson & Johnson, the firm today employs 380. Most are located on the 270-acre Postley Farm on Bear Tavern Road in Hopewell Township, where a new complex of research labs, manufacturing, warehousing, and administrative offices were dedicated on June 9, 1972. Under the leadership of George H. Luber, who assumed the presidency of Pitman-Moore, Inc., in January 1984, the company continues to be a leader in the development of new veterinary products.

Pitman-Moore, Inc., Washington Crossing, New Jersey.

THE TRENTON TIMES

First editions of the afternoon Trenton Times, *the morning* New Jersey State Gazette, *and the weekly* Trenton Sunday Advertiser *appear at top, and 1929 editions at bottom.*

A centennial-year edition of The Trenton Times.

On a Monday morning early in February 1903, reporter James Kerney—as usual—was not on hand at *The Trenton Times* office at the appointed hour of 8:30 a.m. City editor Walter Fox Allen read the riot act. "This sort of thing," he said of his tardy star reporter, "has got to stop. There will be no favoritism in this office."

Then, as Allen would later recall: "I looked at the *State Gazette* and discovered that Mr. Kerney had bought an interest in the *Times* and was my boss. There was no more reading of the riot act that morning."

The first, four-page issue of *The Trenton Times* was published on October 12, 1882. The *Times* printed the most important news—local as well as national and world—on the front page at a time when competitors still used it largely for ads. That policy set it apart and, aided by several libel suits, it gained a reputation for daring reporting.

But advertisers were unimpressed.

Founder Lawrence S. Mott, who had wanted to challenge the older *State Gazette* and *True American,* lost heart and the paper passed to its chief debtor, the printer. Several owners and locations followed, so that in 1900, when a three-man team took over to modernize and reorganize, they were the seventh owners.

All of which brings us back to James Kerney, one of the reporters hired for the new staff. As it became clear that the Irishman with an eighth-grade education—soon to be the editor—was at the *Times* to stay, the paper began taking on some of his own character. Not physically a big man, the impression he left was oversize. He used the paper to needle officials, to conduct building campaigns, and to force transit fat cats to back down on raising prices.

In May 1906 the *Times* purchased the building at 10 South Stockton Street, which remained its home for 55 years. In 1912 Kerney bought the *Sunday Advertiser,* changing its name to the *Sunday Times-Advertiser* and printing it as a separate paper. The following year, he merged the old *True American* into the *Times.* He acquired the *State Gazette* in 1926; it

was printed separately until 1942.

He died in 1934, victim of a massive heart attack at the age of 61. Ownership passed to his widow and then to their children, who found they had inherited too small a printing plant. As part of the city's redevelopment, the *Times* acquired land in Coalport and constructed the building that still houses it, moving in on July 2, 1961.

With two of the six Kerney children deceased, the four survivors in 1974 sold the paper to *The Washington Post,* which expanded national news coverage and brought color photography to the paper. Beginning in 1951, *The Trenton Times* returned to an emphasis on local and state news coverage, expanding and strengthening color photography and graphics. Shortly after the paper's 99th anniversary, it was sold to Allbritton Communications Company, the owner also of two other New Jersey dailies, *The Hudson Dispatch* and *The Paterson News.*

By its 100th birthday the *Times* had successfully completed its conversion to morning publication, offering readers four sections daily and twice that number on Sunday. The only thing that hasn't changed is the front page, which is still devoted to news.

BACKES, WALDRON & HILL

John Backes immigrated to America from Germany in 1848, finding work as a blacksmith at Cooper, Hewitt & Co.'s rolling mill. He married Mary Hannes, from his hometown of Trier. The father of six, he died in 1874 from injuries sustained two years earlier in an explosion at the mill.

Peter, the eldest, who was 16 when his father died, worked for a furniture dealer, while the third son, John H., 13, became an office boy for attorney Edward H. Murphy. After reading law with Murphy, John was admitted to the bar in 1884.

Peter then joined Murphy at a time when the lawyer was interested in developing the shore town of Point Pleasant. While John ran the law office in Trenton, Peter worked with the older man at the shore. After his admittance to the bar in 1886, he joined his brother in practice.

Five of the six Backes sons went on to distinguished legal careers: John H. served the New Jersey Court of Chancery for 21 years as a vice-chancellor, Theodore was assistant attorney general, William J. served as advisory master in chancery, and Albert practiced law in Newark.

Peter, who maintained a private practice in Trenton for 55 years, took his son, Herbert W., as a partner in 1913, calling the firm Backes & Backes; his other son, William Wright Backes, joined them in 1930.

Longtime clients include New Jersey National Bank, New Jersey Manufacturers Insurance Company, Transamerica Delaval Inc., Morton Thiokol, Inc., Roller-Bearing Company of America, Goodall Rubber, and the Trenton Saving Fund Society, while the Catholic Diocese of Trenton has been represented by the firm since 1886. Backes & Backes served as counsel to John A. Roebling's Sons Company in the 1954 sale to Colorado Fuel & Iron, just as it had earlier represented the Maddock Pottery during its acquisition by American Standard in 1929.

When he died in December 1941, Peter had already welcomed Herbert's son, Robert Maddock Backes, into the family firm. A second grandson, William W. Backes, Jr., followed in 1966. In 1954 James A. Waldron became the first non-Backes to join the firm, followed four years later by Harry R. Hill, Jr. Together with the two third-generation family members, they make up the four partners of the firm known since 1980 as Backes, Waldron & Hill.

Robert M. Backes, James A. Waldron, and Harry R. Hill, Jr., are all former presidents of the Mercer County Bar Association. Their firm represents Mercer Medical Center, of which Robert M. Backes is a former president and on whose board William W. Backes, Jr., now serves, as well as St. Francis Medical Center, where James A. Waldron is an advisory board member. Michael J. Nizolek, Robert C. Billmeier, Thomas M. Brown, and Brenda F. Engel are associated in the firm's practice.

From 1892 until 1925 Peter Backes' offices were located in the Forst-Richey Building at State and Warren; Backes & Backes in 1925 became the first tenant to move into the new Trenton Trust Building at

From 1892 until 1925 the Backes law offices were located at State and Warren, in the Forst-Richey Building. Courtesy of the Trentoniana Collection, Trenton Free Public Library.

28 West State Street. In 1984 the firm plans to move to new quarters at 15 West Front Street.

Long a force in city legal affairs, Backes, Waldron & Hill has grown with Mercer County for almost a century, from a small 19th-century law office to one of the area's leading law firms.

Peter Backes, Esq.

RITCHIE & PAGE DISTRIBUTING COMPANY

Founded as a coal company on Pennington Road during the Great Depression, Ritchie & Page was reorganized as a beer wholesaler, with offices and a warehouse on Perrine Avenue, following Prohibition's 1933 repeal. During the '30s and '40s R&P dealt in such colorful but now-defunct brands as Eblings, Peter Bright, Pride of Newark, Rheingold, Sunshine, and Hoffman.

Both George W. Page and Arthur W. Ritchie were highly visible members of the community throughout their careers. Ritchie was the businessman of the combination and so was widely known in tavern and package-store circles; Page was a popular politician who held several elective and appointive offices, most notably as a city commissioner and as warden of Trenton State Prison.

In 1949 these men made a decision that changed the course of the company and assured its success: They took on the products of Anheuser Busch, a St. Louis brewer trying to establish a national beer market. At the time, Anheuser Busch had only one brewery, a very small northeastern market, and two brands of beer, Budweiser and Michelob. It has since grown to 11 enormous breweries across the country, and now generates sales that annually set beer-industry records.

However, success did not come immediately or easily for Ritchie & Page. The company grew slowly in the '50s by selling Schmidts beer as well as Anheuser Busch products. The firm moved to its present location at 292 Third Street in 1953.

An unprecedented period of sustained growth and success

followed the 1963 acquisition of Ritchie & Page by a former Anheuser Busch executive, Thomas J. Ryan, and his brother-in-law, Louis A. Natale, Jr. Under Ryan's leadership, the firm began an aggressive marketing program designed to establish Budweiser and Michelob as the dominant brands of beer in Mercer and Burlington counties. Beginning with approximately three percent of the beer market in 1963, Ryan's program resulted in 20 consecutive annual sales increases, with Anheuser Busch products accounting for more than half the beer sold in the Trenton area by 1983.

During this period of growth and prosperity, Ritchie & Page made a commitment to Trenton's institutions and people. While the '60s and '70s was an era when Trenton businessmen moved or closed at an alarming rate, Ritchie & Page maintained the philosophy that a company should "put something

back" into the community where it conducts its business.

Consistent with this philosophy, all corporate expansion has been accomplished in the Third Street neighborhood. Between 1972 and 1982 two major warehouses were erected, a large office building renovated, and a two-acre parking lot cleared. During this process, a number of old and abandoned Scammel Pottery and Resolute China buildings, which had deteriorated into fire and health hazards, were torn down and replaced by modern, functional structures.

With the 1983 observance of the company's 50th year of service to Trenton, the people at Ritchie & Page are working to make the next half-century a rebirth of prosperity and success for the city.

The main office of Ritchie & Page Distributing Company at 292 Third Street was originally constructed in 1926 and completely renovated in 1975.

NEW JERSEY MANUFACTURERS INSURANCE COMPANY

Passage of the New Jersey Workmen's Compensation Act in 1911 prompted members of the Manufacturers Association of the State of New Jersey (known today as the New Jersey Business and Industry Association) to seek an efficient way of fulfilling their obligations as employers to employees injured in job-connected accidents. Concerned with the prospect of the high premiums that might be charged by some insurers, a special association committee studied the matter and recommended the establishment of a new insurance company that would provide effective services and quality protection to the membership at an economical cost. Experience gained from the experimentation that followed was incorporated into the

From 1920 to 1947 the New Jersey Manufacturers Insurance Company made 175 West State Street its headquarters. The structure was erected in 1874 as a residence for John H. Stewart, a well-known lawyer and Mercer County judge.

design of the New Jersey Manufacturers Casualty Insurance Company, which commenced operation in June 1913.

To make that company unique among its competitors, intricate safeguards were devised to assure that its operation would always be for the exclusive benefit of its policyholders. In 1918, after gaining sufficient expertise and attaining satisfactory reserves, capital, and surplus, this spirit of mutuality was given substance by payment of the first dividend to customers at the rate of 20 percent of premium. Regular dividends at rates never lower have since been returned or credited to voluntarily insured policyholders each year without interruption.

To provide protection necessitated by the widespread use of motor vehicles, the Casualty Insurance Company offered auto liability insurance starting in 1917. To complement the coverage with protection against loss or damage to an insured's own property, New Jersey Manufacturers Association Fire Insurance Company was formed in 1921. Four years later New Jersey Manufacturers Association Hospitals, Inc., was organized to provide a vehicle to fulfill the notion that job-related injuries could be better managed if treated quickly by medical specialists at clinics convenient to the job site.

The year 1951 saw the transformation of the Fire Insurance Company into New Jersey Manufacturers Indemnity Insurance Company, which had broadened powers. The Hospitals Company was dissolved in 1956 and its functions

Since 1966 the NJM organizations have made their principal home at this Sullivan Way complex.

absorbed by the Medical Department of the Casualty Insurance Company. Further consolidation followed in 1965 when the Casualty and Indemnity Companies were merged into the present New Jersey Manufacturers Insurance Company, which was authorized to write virtually all property-casualty coverages. More recently, New Jersey Re-Insurance Company was added as an NJM subsidiary in 1977. The new carrier is licensed to conduct property-casualty insurance and reinsurance operations.

New Jersey Manufacturers Insurance Company has emerged from modest beginnings to become the state's predominant liability and property insurance carrier. It is now the leading workers' compensation insurer, the second-largest writer of auto coverages, and numbers among the top 10 providers of homeowners' policies. With a work force exceeding 1,500, most of whom are located at the Sullivan Way complex, NJM has grown to be one of the largest employers in the Trenton area.

UNION CAMP CORPORATION

Union Camp Corporation has manufactured corrugated containers at its East State Street plant since 1947. The 165,000-square-foot facility employs 125 people.

Before the Civil War, storekeepers wrapped the merchandise they sold in paper and string bundles. But in 1861 a Bethlehem, Pennsylvania, teacher named Francis Wolle—who already held a patent on a machine to make paper bags—enlisted enough financial backing to form the Union Paper Bag Machine Company, a forerunner of Union Camp.

The availability of ready-made paper bags in a variety of sizes altered

Union Camp employees operate machinery which makes corrugated board from huge rolls of kraft paperboard, like the one pictured here.

the customer's transport problems. But shipping remained expensive for the manufacturer well after the production of the first single-wall corrugated boxes in 1894, because the railroads charged a premium rate for their use. Not until the rate penalties were overturned on the eve of World War I did the corrugated industry begin its dramatic growth.

Union Camp—the result of the 1956 merger of Union Bag and Paper Corporation and Camp Manufacturing Company, Inc.—ranks in the top half of the country's 500 largest industrial corporations. A forest-products company with over 17,000 employees whose operations are concentrated in the eastern third of the country, Union Camp is headquartered in Wayne, and it has three plants elsewhere in the state in addition to its corporate research center near Princeton. Its 25 container plants alone employ 3,000 people in the United States.

But in 1947, when Union Camp came to Trenton, it was just entering the box business. Until then, the company had supplied linerboard

and medium to box makers, but in that year it built a plant on the site of its paper mill in Savannah and bought two others, in Trenton and Chicago.

In addition to acquiring the Trenton Container Company, which had been producing corrugated boxes since 1936, Union Camp bought a vacant factory across from it, at 1400 East State Street. Transformed by the addition of the best available equipment, it became one of the first highly mechanized corrugated plants in the country.

Much of the kraft board used in Trenton is manufactured at Union Camp's kraft paper mill at Savannah, and shipped north by inland coastal waterway to Paulsboro, before being trucked to East State Street. There, within the 165,000-square-foot plant, the linerboard and medium are laminated together to form corrugated board, which is then printed, slotted, folded, and glued into containers. In a trend that is reflected throughout the firm, 21 percent of the Trenton plant's 125 employees have been with Union Camp for 30 years or more.

Like the company's other container plants, Trenton services local as well as national clients, who are attracted by Union Camp's capability to design and manufacture high-quality containers which meet demanding strength, cost, and handling specifications. Major national clients are Procter & Gamble, Anchor-Hocking, and Johns-Manville, while American-Standard, Ocean Spray, Original Trenton Crackers, and Sterling Drug lead the list of local customers.

SQUIBB CORPORATION

Medicines were still being sold under vague descriptions and without tested standards of purity or potency in the mid-19th century, when an assistant naval surgeon began lobbying for drug purity.

Heeding the arguments of Dr. Edward Robinson Squibb, Congress in 1852 established a drug research laboratory at the Brooklyn Naval Yard. Working with equipment he had designed, Dr. Squibb tested drugs and worked to find an improved method of distilling ether. In 1856 he published his method of distilling the world's first effective and controllable anesthetic.

He resigned from the Navy the following year to establish his own laboratory near the naval yard. Despite a disastrous fire there in which he was badly burned, Dr. Squibb had set up his manufacturing lab by the end of 1859, and acted as a major supplier of ether and drugs to the Union Army during the Civil War. A relentless campaigner for drug standards, he established a proposal in 1879 that was a model for subsequent state legislation and the 1906 federal food and drug act.

In the years since Dr. Squibb's death in 1899, the company he established has expanded into a worldwide manufacturer of health care products used by over

300 million people in more than 120 countries. Decisions made today at Squibb's corporate headquarters in Lawrence Township guide research, production, and marketing activities for nearly 1,000 products serving almost every specialty of medical care.

Research and development, the foundations of Dr. Squibb's pioneering work, remain central to the company's efforts. The Squibb Institute for Medical Research, also headquartered at the Lawrence Township facility, was established in 1938 as the first industry-sponsored organization of its kind. The Institute now employs some 1,000 scientists and technicians around the world.

The Institute has been home base for such distinguished scientists as Dr. Oskar Paul Wintersteiner, who spearheaded Squibb's successful search for a stable and producible strain of penicillin in the 1940s, leading to the 1944 opening by Squibb of the largest penicillin production plant in the world, at New Brunswick. Current Institute members include Drs. Miguel Ondetti and David Cushman, who led the 10-year effort that in 1981 developed Capoten, an enzyme inhibitor that has proved safe and effective against both hypertension and the symptoms of congestive heart failure; and Drs. Richard Sykes and Chris Cimarusti, who were instrumental in the 1981 discovery of monobactams, a new class of antibiotics whose structure

A major breakthrough in the conquest of infectious disease took place at Squibb laboratories in June 1943, when the late Dr. Oskar Wintersteiner isolated the sodium salt of penicillin providing, at last, a standard for testing.

was suggested by bacteria found in soil from the New Jersey Pine Barrens.

The firm was sold in 1905 by the founder's children to Lowell M. Palmer and Theodore Weicker. Fifty years later Squibb was acquired by the Mathieson Chemical Company, and remained part of Olin-Mathieson Corporation until 1968, when it merged with BeechNut Life Savers to form a diversified food and drug concern. With the 1981 disposal of Life Savers, Squibb's only non-health care business is the New York-based Charles of the Ritz personal care products.

In 1972 the worldwide headquarters of E.R. Squibb & Sons, Inc., moved to a complex of 11 interconnected buildings situated on 273 acres on Route 206 in Lawrence Township. A decade later plans were announced to relocate the parent corporation's headquarters to the same site and to expand its facilities there.

The award-winning world headquarters of Squibb Corporation, near Princeton, New Jersey.

PEGASUS INTERNATIONAL CORPORATION

The business of Pegasus International Corporation is technology transfer, the licensing of products and processes overseas, export and import marketing, and arranging and managing joint ventures worldwide. Branch offices are located around the globe.

Pegasus was founded in 1951 by Andrew Wolff, Paul Weill, and Allan Conwill to sell American technical know-how to Asia and Europe. The company prospered and became part of ASPRO, a conglomerate, in order to service its member firms internationally.

In 1974, when ASPRO decided to sell Pegasus, Win Straube, manager of the company at the time, became the sole owner of the New York-based firm. He decided to relocate Pegasus to Central New Jersey in 1976 and purchased a turn-of-the-century brick and stone building complex in Pennington that—over the years—had housed a variety of manufacturing firms. He since has guided the renovation of the complex into an international research and office park.

A book, *Straube Center USA,* written by journalist Donna Amick and published in 1982, tells in detail the history of "the old foundry building" and its place in America's industrial history.

Straube Center is dominated not by buildings, but by shade trees, shrubbery, and lawns. Its focus is a giant apple tree, emphasizing the philosophy of Pegasus: sensitivity to the rest of the world, the pursuit of excellence rooted in solid knowledge, and appreciation of nature and its ways.

In 1980 Pegasus launched a separate division that offers "art you can touch": limited-edition bronze sculptures by renowned artists. The company sees this as a cultural contribution to the community.

Pegasus International's resource is people. To work there an employee must be at home in three languages: English; Japanese, German, Spanish, or any other; and computer. As part of today's computer-based society, the Pegasus staff is a group of professionals working without secretaries, running a network of international commerce: WINDOW TO THE WORLD.

Straube Center, *an oil painting by John Gummere, 1982.*

BARBERO BAKERY, INC.

When Gerardo Barbero left the province of Avelino for America in 1903, he had never heard of Trenton and had no thought of becoming a baker. Intent on making money, he worked three years in Haverstraw, New York, as a brick maker before returning for three years to his native Montemarano, where he married.

Most of the next four years he spent in Haverstraw—where new friends nicknamed him "Cholly"—visiting Italy and his family when he could. Caught at home when war was declared, he returned in 1921 to work at a cousin's Boston grocery.

In 1924 he moved to Trenton and took up a new trade, learning the bakery business at the Breccia Brothers Bakery on Roebling Avenue. When he left in 1925 to open his own place at 61 Conrad Street, he took no chances: His partner was an experienced baker, the business was called the French Italian Bakery, and the Americanized Barbero signed himself Charles.

The first partner returned to Italy after two years and was replaced by another baker, who left in 1929. The sole owner, Cholly Barbero finally felt able to send for his wife, Maria, and children, Angelo, Nina, and Armando.

Angelo, who was not quite 14 when he arrived, recalls that the bakery made only two or three kinds of Italian bread. With his father at the wheel, their Model T delivery truck stopped at neighborhood homes to collect the housewife's dough, which would be shaped and baked to her liking. During the Depression, the baking of homemade dough accounted for half the business, with bakery sales supplemented by a truck route to small stores around the city.

The war years were so hard that the bakery barely survived: In July 1945 the Barberos stopped delivering to all but stores in the immediate neighborhood because of the shortage of help. But within six months after V-J Day, they had regained all the contracts. A third truck was added in 1946, and the following year the bakery introduced a sweet line. Armando, the second son, went away to the Dunwood Baking Institute in 1949, and the pastry line was increased when he returned.

The children formed a new corporation when Cholly Barbero retired in 1955. Armando left the next year to establish his own business, and in 1964 Nina and her husband sold out to Angelo. With his son, Gerard, he expanded wholesale deliveries.

Angelo, who began working at the bakery in 1929 and had worked there full time since 1933, and his wife Rose, who had worked part time since their marriage in 1938 and full time since 1947, visited Italy in 1966. While they renewed acquaintances in Montemarano—which neither had seen since emigrating as children—their son ran the bakery. In 1972 he rebuilt and expanded it, adding a deli department, grocery items, and a bigger pastry line.

With their trucks now servicing 10 wholesale routes and several retail stores, the Barberos employ 85 people. They have opened additional satellite bakeries at the Trenton Farmers' Market and in Hamilton Square. Two of Cholly Barbero's five great-grandchildren are learning the trade he finally settled on, and one, Gerard Jr., recently graduated from the Dunwood Baking Institute and the Wilton Decorating School in Chicago.

Armando Barbero (in cap) poses outside the bakery in the early '50s with helpers and his nephew Gerard (front, right).

Angelo Barbero, who became sole owner of the family bakery in 1964, began helping his father in 1929 and started as a full-time baker in 1933.

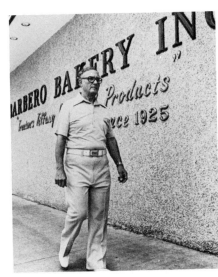

AMERICAN STANDARD INC.

Trenton's first major pottery was built in 1852; a decade later there were 10, and by 1893 the city could boast 37 potteries. While American-Standard didn't come to town until 1929, the origins of its Klockner Road plant go back to 19th-century England and Thomas Maddock.

Born into a family of Staffordshire potters, Maddock served his apprenticeship as a chinaware decorator in Longport before immigrating to this country in 1847. He established a china-decorating business in New York City and worked as a salesman until, in 1873, he joined the Trenton earthenware firm of Millington and Ashbury as a partner. He was interested in producing ceramic plumbing fixtures, then imported from England for the wealthy few.

His idea was no small challenge: Two earlier attempts by American potteries had ended in failure. Too much flint produced cracking; too much feldspar gave the body a glassy character that tended to bend and craze; if the kiln temperature wasn't properly regulated, the ware warped out of shape. Pottery workers had been paid according to the number of usable pieces removed from the kilns, but even that standard had to change since as much as 90 percent of the early production was unusable.

Maddock did all the selling himself. A man who never wore an overcoat or carried an umbrella, he walked from one prospective buyer to another in Lower Manhattan, carrying his heavy wares tied up in muslin. Late in 1873 he made his first sale. His wares carried the British coat of arms and the words: "Best

Thomas Maddock's Sons Company, purchased by the Standard Sanitary Manufacturing Company in 1929, was at that time the largest factory in America devoted exclusively to the manufacture of vitreous china plumbing fixtures.

Staffordshire Earthenware made for the American market." The American sanitary-ware industry had begun.

Although his first basins and toilets couldn't compare with the quality of English ware, Maddock was nonetheless a success. He was without American competitors until 1879, when the Enterprise Pottery Company was founded in Trenton. In 1880 he was granted a patent for the first satisfactory connection of a toilet with the flushing-water supply, and three years later Maddock produced the first domestic sanitary pottery catalog. Until 1892 Trenton was the only city in the country producing sanitary ware.

Following Maddock's death in 1899, his four sons reincorporated as

Thomas Maddock's Sons Company and in 1924-1925 built a huge new plant on Klockner Road in Hutchinson's Mills. In 1929 the Maddocks approached the Standard Sanitary Manufacturing Company to buy enameled cast-iron baths. Standard, however, became interested in the Maddock operation, buying the company in September, weeks before the stock market collapse. That same year saw the merger of the American Radiator Company with Standard Sanitary, creating the corporation now known as American-Standard, the world's largest producer of plumbing fixtures.

Over the years, 28 million pieces of sanitary plumbing ware have been produced at the Klockner Road plant, where a recent expansion program has increased the firing capacity by 50 percent. Long one of the Trenton area's largest employers, American-Standard remains committed to Thomas Maddock's vision of a great domestic industry.

Early samples of Thomas Maddock's Sons Company's products were displayed in catalogs.

CAPITOL STATE BANK

A Chambersburg branch bank opened on Chambers Street in 1976.

Opened in 1975, the bank's South Broad Street headquarters is on the site of the Second Battle of Trenton.

In December 1972, 56 incorporators asked New Jersey's state banking commissioner to charter a new downtown Trenton bank. The applicants—none of whom invested more than $50,000—described themselves as representatives of business and professional interests in the Trenton area who were "dedicated to the idea of bringing renewed vitality to downtown Trenton," and who wanted "to give small businessmen, minority groups, and others an opportunity to invest in Trenton's future."

The bank they proposed had a capitalization of $2.25 million, the largest sum presented for a state bank up to that time. Chartered in September 1973, Capitol State Bank in April 1974 bought a $58,555 half-acre lot at 100 South Broad Street, part of the Mercer-Jackson redevelopment project. The following month the new bank opened for business in a double trailer across South Broad Street from its permanent site.

Its 8,000-square-foot, $800,000 facility was officially opened on December 15, 1975, a year to the day after bank officers turned over a check for the land at a city hall ceremony. After 18 months in its trailer office, the new bank reported assets of $15 million, with deposits running 100 percent ahead of initial projections.

State approval of plans to build a Chambersburg branch was announced by bank president Philip A. Kerner on the first day of business at the bank's new headquarters. Located at 695 Chambers Street, the branch bank opened in March 1976.

In addition to its 10-man board of directors, Capitol State Bank is guided by a 15-person advisory board. The desire of both boards to involve the bank in its community was reflected in the institution's 1980 sponsorship of a charity ball to benefit the Sister Georgine Learning Center for exceptional children. Now an annual winter event, subsequent balls have raised funds for St. Francis Hospital in 1981 and Villa Victoria Academy in 1982—a total of $39,000 for the three nonprofit institutions. The 1983 ball was dedicated to the War Memorial Building restoration fund.

In January 1983 Frank J. Gubitose was named president of the bank, having served as vice-president since the previous July. The board of directors he joined includes seven of the original nine members—Robert J. Greer, chairman of the board; Louis J. Crecco; Walter B. Hankin; Carl F. Jacobelli; Carl Kaplan; Vincent B. Pica, M.D.; and William H. Thompson, D.D.S. New members are Robert C. Maida, Esq., son of the late chairman of the board, Nicholas C. Maida; and Russell J. Snyder.

As it enters its 10th year, Capitol State Bank is the sort of institution its incorporators hoped for: a small, independent bank, offering personalized service to its depositors.

FIRST PRESBYTERIAN CHURCH

The history of the First Presbyterian Church, founded in 1712, is inextricably woven in Trenton's past. This Greek revival-style structure was begun in 1839, incorporating all salvageable material from the previous church.

The beginnings of the First Presbyterian Church date to 1712, but it was not until 1726 that a small church of native stone was built on the southwest corner of the present church lot. On September 8, 1756, First Presbyterian was incorporated under a charter from King George II.

During the Revolution the church was damaged, many of its records lost or destroyed, and its manse occupied as a Hessian hospital. Following the Battle of Trenton, the Hessian commander, Colonel Johann Gottlieb Rall, was buried in an unmarked grave in the churchyard, along with a number of his soldiers. John Adams attended services on September 20, 1777, and on October 27, 1781, the first news of

the surrender at Yorktown was celebrated in services attended by the governor and legislature.

The Old Stone Church was taken down in 1805 to make room for a brick church, dedicated on August 17, 1806. President James Monroe attended services in that church on June 8, 1817, and General Lafayette worshipped there on September 26, 1824.

In 1839, when plans were made to erect the present church, its site was moved to the center of the property, facing East State Street. All salvageable materials from the earlier church were used in the new Greek revival-style building, including the base of Jersey sandstone. The walls above it are brick, stuccoed on the exterior and plastered inside.

First Presbyterian has a long history of involvement outside of its own congregation. In 1839 the church welcomed its first black member, Thomas Wilson, who became a missionary in Liberia. A second black member was ordained in 1846. In 1887 the church assumed support of a missionary in India, and the following year contributed to the building of a church in Carthage, North Carolina, while beginning special Sunday evening classes for Trenton's Oriental citizens. The congregation has since helped support missionaries in China and Korea, an Arizona Indian reservation, and a New Mexico hospital.

In 1975 the church began a half-day nursery school which soon grew into a year-round day care center for children of the working poor. Located in one of the buildings the church owns on the East Hanover

This classic 19th-century church, with its elegantly simple interior, contains one of the finest pipe organs in the state.

Street side of its lot, the center has gradually expanded into a school as well, opened formally as the Trenton Academy in the fall of 1983, with 45 children in kindergarten through second grade, and plans to expand by one grade a year. As another part of its commitment to the inner city, in 1983 the church initiated a 24-hour crisis and referral service, called the Hanover Street Ministry, in cooperation with Christ Episcopal Church of Trenton and Nassau Presbyterian and Trinity Episcopal churches of Princeton.

First Presbyterian Church's endowments have made possible not only the school and street ministry, but a mid-week series of mission programs also aimed at those outside the congregation. These include a worship service, Bible study, a First Friday seminar, and a Wednesday cinema supper club, open to those who would otherwise be eating alone.

Just as its early history is inseparable from that of the town growing up around it, so the modern First Presbyterian Church sees itself as a committed part of the city of Trenton.

CRECCO'S RESTAURANT

In September 1947, when Lorenzo and Cecelia Crecco and their son, Louis, opened a neighborhood bar, they had no plans for a restaurant. The corner saloon they established at Morris and Anderson streets was a workingman's place—a shot-and-beer drinker's bar that first offered sandwiches, and later tomato pies and pasta.

Lorenzo Crecco, called Larry, was

helped by reviews in magazines and newspapers in New York and Philadelphia.

But while it continues to attract diners from all over, it remains very much a Trenton gathering place, one with a large number of loyal customers who speak of it as not only a restaurant, but a social club.

That atmosphere has been heightened through the years by the

midnight Saturday dinners for "family customers," hosted first by Larry and continued by Lou. Politicians, policemen, sportswriters, railroad engineers, lawyers, and doctors get together with their families and friends at these weekly gatherings, sharing a common table that may seat as many as 30 or as few as eight on any given week.

The elder Creccos retired in 1963, eventually moving to Jacksonville, Florida, where Larry died in 1982. Their son, who still lives above the family business, is a golfer and marathon runner and has played host to many sports figures at the family restaurant.

Years ago an advertising agency prepared a campaign for Crecco's that consisted of small congratulatory messages, each ending, "Best regards, L.C." Used to honor customers' achievements, the ads have called attention to the restaurant's clientele for a quarter of a century. As the autographed pictures that line the dining room walls attest, people as varied as Paul Whiteman, John Wayne, and Gerald Ford have left behind their praise of Crecco's.

Echoing his own customers, the proprietor says he couldn't imagine his life without Crecco's.

Lorenzo "Larry" Crecco (right) opened this corner saloon in 1947. With no plans for a restaurant at that time, he was assisted in serving drinks and sandwiches by his wife Jessie (center) and son Lou (left).

born in Ribi, 12 kilometers south of Rome. He had been the assistant brewmaster at the Trenton Brewing Company, makers of Trenton Old Stock beer, before starting his own business. His wife, the former Cecelia DiLouie, called Jessie, used family recipes as customers began to ask for a more varied menu. Their son, Lou, who had been a pilot with the Army Air Corps during World War II, added a fourth member to the family staff 18 months after the business opened, when he married Marian.

The small family bar has expanded over two properties and become a Trenton institution in the intervening years. Emphasizing top-quality ingredients and homemade sauces, Crecco's has seen its reputation grow over a wide area,

Lou Crecco (right) carries on the family tradition begun by his father. Crecco's Restaurant is still a gathering place for local residents and celebrities alike. Here he and wife Marian greet Joe DiMaggio (center), ex-New York Yankee baseball great.

BEITEL DISPLAYS, INC.

After World War II, towns across America began showing off their local businesses in home shows. Space in the local armory was divided among participating companies, many of which brought their in-house display men—window dressers, art department personnel, or industrial designers—to assemble and arrange the exhibits. As trade shows became more sophisticated, the demand for professional exhibit designers and producers increased greatly.

Today's trade shows have evolved into showcases for as many as 1,200 exhibiting companies at one time, with the cost of many of the exhibits used ranging in the tens of thousands of dollars. In 1983 there were over 9,000 trade shows in the United States alone. The Beitel Company specializes in engineering its clients' exhibit requirements to produce attractive and functional exhibit units. A completed unit will have passed through every skilled department from design through the carpenter shop and silkscreening. Beitel's 26 employees serve some 350 clients, and its staff carpenters provide installation and dismantling services for client exhibits at show sites throughout the country.

What is now Beitel Displays had its origins in the small North Stockton Street advertising agency Geo. W. Brown started in 1928. When Brown retired in 1952, William J. Beitel, a 20-year employee of the firm, bought its display department.

Joined by his wife, Mary, and son, Wm. J.J. Beitel, he moved the business to South Broad Street, near Liberty; then to Franklin Street in

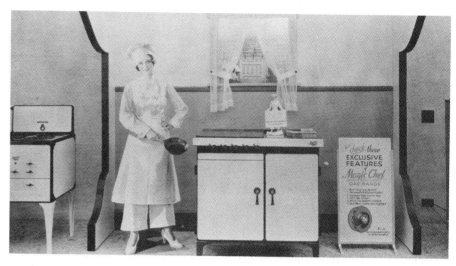

A typical exhibit produced by William J. Beitel and used at early "home shows" across the country.

Chambersburg; and in 1971 to 354 South Broad Street. Each move was caused by the need for more space, as the Beitel family business grew with its industry.

In 1963 the younger Beitel moved from the construction side of the family business to sales, joining his father as a partner. Since the retirement of his parents in 1974, Wm. J.J. Beitel has been the president and sole corporate proprietor.

When New Jersey got into the lottery business in 1978, so did Beitel. The machine that chooses the winning number for Garden State lottery players—familiar to millions from a live show telecast six days a week—attracted the interest of Delaware, Illinois, Maryland, New York, Pennsylvania, Rhode Island, and Washington, D.C., all of them now Beitel customers.

The company's more serious side can be seen in the reception lobby of the Princeton Plasma Physics Laboratory, the wall graphics and interior signs for St. Francis Medical Center, and the Mobile Information Center for the state Department of

Labor & Industry. Museum work includes the design, fabrication, and installation of the Afro-American Museum exhibit in Philadelphia, the Hall of Science for the New Jersey State Museum, and display cases for fine porcelains at the Trenton City Museum.

With its 1983 move to 1880 Princeton Avenue in Lawrence Township, the firm commands 15,000 square feet for warehousing clients' exhibits and displays, as well as 25,000 square feet of space for offices and graphics, screen printing, and cabinet shops.

The award-winning 1983 trade show exhibit created by Beitel Displays, Inc., for Boehm Porcelain of Trenton.

ROYAL ENGINEERING COMPANY

The oldest part of Royal Engineering's plant is this two-story brick shop to the rear of Pennington Avenue.

The Royal name is one of the few constants in the early history of the company, founded in 1935 by brothers Barnett and David Rochestie.

What began as a manufacturer of penny scales on Factory Street quickly became a fluorescent lighting fabricator at Bridge and Bloomsbury streets, an electrical repair service on

Only the third story of the late-Victorian house, which the firm acquired in 1942, can be seen above Royal's two-story brick expansion on Pennington Avenue. Courtesy of Lehigh Photographs.

Perry Street, and then a maker of blue and pink baby scales on Samuel Street—all before its 1942 establishment as a metal-stamping concern on Pennington Avenue.

The first name was the Royal Scale Company, but by 1942—the year the firm moved into a late-Victorian house at 330 Pennington Avenue— it had become the Royal Engineering Company.

Royal first entered the display business because Congoleum Industries wanted to place a large order for signs. The company now specializes in metal fabrication and stamping, housing for electronic components, point-of-purchase displays, fixtures, and frames.

In March 1982 Barnett Rochestie sold the enterprise to Stephen S. Alpert Industries, owner also of Samuel Eastman Company, Inc., and Micromelt, Inc., both of Concord, New Hampshire. The acquisition by Alpert has given Royal the added design, engineering, and manufacturing resources of the parent corporation, which is primarily involved in foundry work.

With the purchase of a building at

377 Enterprise Avenue in 1982, Royal Engineering now has total manufacturing and distributing facilities of more than 110,000 square feet; the firm employs 100 workers.

Since its acquisition by Alpert Industries, Royal has announced the development of injection-molded clear plastic frames for use in displaying floor-covering samples. Royal has also become the exclusive U.S. distribution agent for Intertex's space-saving motorized units for the storage, display, and cutting of carpeting and vinyl floor covering.

While Chester Klabbatz, the firm's executive vice-president, and treasurer Robert J. Sweeny agree that Royal is still known primarily for its work in metal stamping, they point with pride to their company's ability to function as designer, developer, and manufacturer of point-of-purchase displays for permanent and semipermanent installation. With the addition of its own computer system, Royal's two divisions—Royal Displays & Fixtures and Royal Metal Fabricators—look forward to their continued ability to offer clients fast and flexible service.

PATRONS

The following individuals, companies, and organizations have made a valuable commitment to the quality of this publication. Windsor Publications and the Trenton Historical Society gratefully acknowledge their participation in *A Capital Place: The Story of Trenton.*

American Biltrite, Inc.*
American Decorators, Inc.*
American Standard Inc.*
Backes, Waldron & Hill*
Barbero Bakery, Inc.*
Base Ten Systems, Inc.*
Beitel Displays, Inc.*
William E. Blackman
Capital State Bank*
Capitol Plaza Hotel, Spirit of Trenton
City of Trenton, NJ
W. Edwin and Dorothy Collier
Crecco's Restaurant*

Frederick W. Donnelly & Son*
Doolan Real Estate Agency
First Presbyterian Church*
Fisne Trucking Company
Free Public Library/Township of Hamilton
Friends of Trenton Free Public Library
   Cadwalader Branch
Helene Fuld Medical Center*
Griffith Electric Supply Company, Inc.*
Heinemann Electric Company*
The R.C. Maxwell Company*
Mercer County Community College*
Mill Supply & Hardware Co., Inc.
New Jersey Bell*
New Jersey Manufacturers Insurance
   Company*
New Jersey National Bank*
New Jersey State Museum, Trenton
Pegasus International Corporation*
Pitman-Moore, Inc.*
Gallus Charles Quigley, Sr.

Rider College*
Ritchie & Page Distributing Company*
Roller Bearing Company of America*
Royal Engineering Company*
H.M. Royal, Incorporated*
St. Francis Medical Center*
Sonic Instruments*
Squibb Corporation*
Switlik Parachute Company, Inc.*
Transamerica Delaval Inc.*
Trenton Artists Workshop Association
   (TAWA)
Trenton Free Public Library
Trenton Sheet Metal, Inc.*
The Trenton Times*
Union Camp Corporation*

*Partners in Progress of *A Capital Place: The Story of Trenton.* The histories of these companies and organizations appear in Chapter 9, beginning on page 117.

Although Dr. James Naismith invented basketball in Springfield, the first professional game was played in Trenton in 1896. A decade later, college and industrial teams developed. The determination to win is reflected in the faces of these players from the Trent Tile Company team of 1902. Courtesy, Trentoniana Collection, TFPL

SOURCES

PUBLISHED SOURCES

Akst, Daniel. "Trenton: Seat of Government and a Study in Contrasts." *The New York Times*, May 3, 1981 (Section 11).

Banks, Ivy Jackson. *Banks of the Delaware: The Life and Times of Frederick Banks, 1898-1964.* Trenton: The Trenton Historical Society, 1967.

Barber, John W., and Howe, Henry. *Historical Collections of the State of New Jersey.* New York: S. Tuttle, 1846.

Benedict, William H. "New Jersey as it Appeared to Early Observers and Travelers." *Proceedings of the New Jersey Historical Society,* New Series, 5 (1920) 153-168.

Bowling, Kenneth R. "A Place to Which Tribute is Brought: The Contest for the Federal Capital in 1783." *Prologue, The Journal of the National Archives,* v.8, no.8 (Fall 1976) 129-139.

Boyer, Charles. *Old Inns and Taverns in West Jersey.* Camden: Camden County Historical Society, 1962.

Butcher, Herbert Borton et al. *History of the Trenton Rotary Club, 1914-1969.* Trenton: The Trenton Historical Society, 1970.

Chastellux, Marquis de. *Travels in North America in the Years 1780, 1781 and 1782.* Revised translation by Howard C. Rice, Jr. 2 v. Chapel Hill: University of North Carolina Press, 1963.

Collins, John. *Reminiscences of Isaac and Rachel (Budd) Collins,. . . .* Philadelphia: J.B. Lippincott Co., 1893.

Felcone, Joseph J., compiler. *Trenton Index. . . .* Princeton: Sheffield Press, 1976.

Fisher, Harriet White. *A Woman's World-Tour in a Motor.* Philadelphia: J.B. Lippincott Co., 1911.

Fitzgerald, Thomas F. *Fitzgerald's Trenton and Mercer County Directory.* Trenton: MacCrellish and Quigley, 1890.

Gerlach, Larry R., editor. *New Jersey in the American Revolution 1763-1783: A Documentary History.* Trenton: New Jersey Historical Commission, 1975.

Godfrey, Carlos E. *The Mechanics Bank, 1834-1919, Trenton in New Jersey, A History.* Privately printed, 1919.

Gordon, Thomas F. *A Gazetteer of the State of New Jersey . . . accompanied by a map.* Trenton: Daniel Fenton, 1834.

————. *The History of New Jersey from its Discovery by Europeans to the Adoption of the Federal Constitution.* Trenton: Daniel Fenton, 1834.

Hall, John. *History of the Presbyterian Church in Trenton, NJ from the first settlement of the town.* 2nd edition. Trenton: MacCrellish and Quigley, 1912. (First edition 1859).

Herman, Hazel. *The Tricentennial Journal: Trenton, New Jersey 1679-1979.* Trenton: City of Trenton, 1979.

Hixson, Richard G. *Isaac Collins, A Quaker Printer in 18th Century America.* New Brunswick: Rutgers University Press, 1968.

Jarrold, Rachel M., and Fromm, Glenn E. *Time the Great Teacher: A History of One Hundred Years of the New Jersey State Teachers College at Trenton, 1855-1955.* Princeton: Princeton University Press, 1955.

Johnston, Howard E. *The Trenton and Mercer Traction Corporation.* Number 26 of The Marker (November 1953) issued by North Jersey Chapter, National Railway Historical Society.

Kalb, Kurt R. et al. "An Urban Ferry Tale." *Bulletin of the Archaeological Society of New Jersey,* No. 38, 1982: 1-17.

Ketchum, Richard M. *The Winter Soldiers.* Garden City, New York: Doubleday & Co., 1973.

Lawrence Historic and Aesthetic Commission. *Historic Land Map of Lawrence (Maidenhead) Township, circa 1776.* Trenton: Trenton Printing Company, 1977.

Maddock, Archibald M., II. *The Polished Earth: A History of the Pottery Plumbing Fixture Industry in the United States.* Trenton: Private publication, 1962.

Memoir of the late Isaac Collins. . . . Philadelphia: Joseph Rakestraw, 1848.

Mercer County. *A Sketch of Mercer County, New Jersey, 1838-1928.* Trenton: Mercer County Board of Chosen Freeholders, 1928.

Muscalus, John A. *Washington's Crossing and the Battle of Trenton, portrayed on Bank Notes, Scrip and Paintings.* Trenton: Private printing, 1972.

Nash, Winona D., and Rizzuto, Neljane. *Minutes of Lawrence (Maidenhead) Township, Mercer County, New Jersey.* v.1. Trenton: Lawrence Historic and Aesthetic Commission, 1976.

Nelson, William. *Beginnings of the Iron Industry in Trenton, New Jersey, 1723-1750.* Philadelphia: Historical Society of Pennsylvania, 1911.

New Jersey State. *27th Annual Report of the Bureau of Statistics of Labor and Industry of New Jersey of the Year Ending October 31st, 1904.* Trenton: MacCrellish and Quigley, State Printers, 1904.

New Jersey State Museum. Catalogs of Exhibitions. "Pottery and Porcelain Made by Ott and Brewer at Etruria Works in Trenton, New Jersey, 1871-1892." Trenton: 1971.

"The American Porcelain Tradition." Trenton: 1971.

"New Jersey Pottery to 1840." Trenton: 1972.

"Eighteenth to Twentieth Century

American Porcelain." Trenton: undated.

"The Pulse of the People: New Jersey 1763-1789." Trenton: 1976.

Nottingham Township. "A Copy of the Minute Book of Nottingham Township, 1692-1710, 1752-1772." *Proceedings of the New Jersey Historical Society*, 58 (1940) 22-44, 124-138, 179-192.

Podmore, Harry J. *Trenton Old and New*. Revised and edited by Mary J. Messler. Trenton: MacCrellish and Quigley Company, 1964.

Potts, Joseph C. *The New Jersey Register for the year 1837: Being the First Year of Publication*. Trenton: William D'Hart, 1837.

Proctor, Mary, and Matuszeski, Bill. *Gritty Cities: A Second Look at . . . Hoboken . . . Paterson . . . Trenton. . . .* Philadelphia: Temple University Press, 1978.

Raum, John O. *History of the City of Trenton, New Jersey*. Trenton: W.T. Nicholson & Co., 1871.

Schuyler, Hamilton. *A History of St. Michael's Church, Trenton*. Princeton: Princeton University Press, 1926.

Schwartz, Joel, and Prosser, Daniel, editors. *Cities of the Garden State: Essays in the Urban and Suburban History of New Jersey*. Dubuque, Iowa: Kendall/ Hunt Publishing Company, 1977.

Shuman, Eleanore Nolan. *The Trenton Story*. Trenton: MacCrellish & Quigley Company, 1958.

Smith, Samuel Stelle. *The Battle of Trenton*. Monmouth Beach: Philip Freneau Press, 1965.

————. *The Battle of Princeton*. Monmouth Beach: Philip Freneau Press, 1967.

Snyder, John P. *The Story of New Jersey's Civil Boundaries, 1609-1968*. Trenton: State Bureau of Geology and Topography, 1969.

Stryker, William S. *The Battles of Trenton and Princeton*. New York: Houghton, Mifflin and Company, 1898. Reprint Spartanburg, South Carolina: The Reprint Company, 1967.

————. *Trenton One Hundred Years Ago*. Privately printed by MacCrellish and

Quigley, Steam Power Book and Job Printers, 1878.

Tomlinson, Paul G. *A History of the Trenton Banking Company 1804-1929*. Princeton: Princeton University Press, 1929.

Trenton Banking Company. *. . . A History of the First Century of its Existence*, prepared by a committee of the Board of Directors. Trenton: MacCrellish and Quigley, 1907.

Trenton Chamber of Commerce. "Trenton: 250th Anniversary of Trenton." Vol. 4, No. 4 *Trenton Magazine*. Trenton: The Kenneth W. Moore Company, 1929.

Trenton City Department of Planning and Development. *An Inventory of Historic Engineering and Industrial Sites, Trenton, New Jersey*. 1977.

Trenton Historical Society. *A History of Trenton 1679-1929*. 2 v. Princeton: Princeton University Press, 1929.

Van Doren, Carl. *Mutiny in January*. New York: The Viking Press, 1943.

Widmer, Kemble. *The Christmas Campaign: The Ten Days of Trenton and Princeton*. Trenton: New Jersey Historical Commission, 1975.

Woodward, Evan M., and Hageman, John F. *History of Burlington and Mercer Counties, New Jersey*. Philadelphia: Everts and Peck, 1883.

ATLASES

Everts and Stewart. *The New Historical Atlas of Mercer County, New Jersey*. Philadelphia: Everts and Stewart, 1875.

Lathrop, J.M. *Atlas of the City of Trenton and Borough of Princeton, Mercer County, New Jersey*. Philadelphia: A.H. Mueller and Co., 1905.

Sanborn, D.A. *Insurance Diagrams of Trenton, New Jersey*. New York: Sanborn Map Co., 1874.

Wolf, George A. *Industrial Trenton and Vicinity*. Wilmington, Delaware: Published by the author, 1900.

NEWSPAPERS

Trenton Times. Bicentennial Issue: Sunday Times Advertiser. July 4, 1976.

Trenton Times. Special Edition. December

23, 1976.

Trenton Times. Trenton: a special edition. October 16, 1979.

The Trentonian. Bill Dwyers's Bygone Days Sampler: Trenton Tricentennial Edition. September 9, 1979.

The Trentonian. The Ten Crucial Days: The Battles of Trenton and Princeton. December 26, 1978.

UNPUBLISHED SOURCES

Cohan, Zara. *"A comprehensive history of the State House of New Jersey and recommendations for its continuation as a historic site."* 1969. Unpublished master's thesis: Newark State College, 1969.

Ewing, Jane. Manuscript Letter. April 23, 1789, Trenton. Manuscript Collection, New Jersey State Archives.

Potts, Stacy Gardiner. *Autobiography*. Manuscript (1859), typescript 1982. New Jersey State Archives.

Prime, Negro. Petition to the Legislature. November 6, 1786, Trenton. Manuscript Collection, New Jersey State Archives.

Toothman, Stephanie S. *"Trenton, New Jersey, 1719-1779: A Study of Community Growth and Organization."* Unpublished doctoral dissertation: University of Pennsylvania, 1977.

Turk, Jessie Rose. *"Trenton, New Jersey in the Nineteenth Century: The Significance of Location in the Historical Geography of a City."* Unpublished doctoral dissertation: Columbia University, 1965.

Wells, Rachel. Petition to the Legislature. November 1785, Bordentown. Manuscript Collection, New Jersey State Archives.

————. Petition to the Legislature. October 26, 1787. Trenton. Manuscript Collection, New Jersey State Archives.

————. Will 1790. September 17, 1795, Bordentown, Burlington County (filed March 23, 1796). New Jersey State Archives.

Zimmerman, Albright G. *"The Indian Trade of Colonial Pennsylvania."* Unpublished doctoral dissertation: University of Delaware, 1966.

INDEX

Italicized numbers indicate illustrations.

158